The
God
Factor

Ignite Your Potential

James Giles

PUBLISHING

The God Factor

James Giles

Unless otherwise noted, Scripture quotations are taken from the King James Version of the Bible. Scripture quotations marked NIV are taken from the New International Version. Copyright 1973, 1978, 1984, International Bible Society. Scripture quotations marked Amplified are taken from the Amplified Old Testament, copyright 1962, 1964, Zondervan Publishing House and from the Amplified New Testament, copyright 1954, 1958, The Lockman Foundation.

Copyright © 1995 James Giles
Printed in the United States of America
ISBN: 1-56229-429-6

Pneuma Life Publishing
P. O. Box 10612
Bakersfield, CA 93389
(805) 324-1741

Table Of Contents

Acknowledgement
Foreword
Preface

Chapter   **Page**

Acknowledgements

To the Father, the Son, and the Holy Spirit. Keep working on me until Christ is completely formed in me.

To my wife Shelley and our four sons, Cedric, Armand, Stephen, and Langston for allowing me to research and write. To Mom and Dad, especially Dad, James Leon Giles, for being there in the clutch and for being the most enthusiastic supporters of my books.

To my uncle, Robert F. Cook, for threatening me in my wayward days. Thanks!

To Keith Byars, come back "string" and have the best season ever. Continue being a positive leader in professional sports.

To Keith Jackson, much success in Green Bay. You're still All-Pro.

To Tony and Renee Morris, for your vision and for all the support and encouragement.

To Alvin and Martha Jones, for your friendship and encouragement (IDLACNAP)!

To Fred Hammond, John P. Kee, Anointed, Yolanda Adams, Commissioned, and Bebe and CeCe Winans, for the gift of song and encouragement.

To Harold and Brenda Ray, for your commitment to excellence.

To New Vision Christian Center, for being bold and daring and for always allowing me to stretch them.

Foreword

The Body of Christ needs to be awakened to a sad and ironic reality. That is, for the most part we failed in our essential purpose: taking dominion of, and reinvigorating the earth with the nature and character of God.

For far too many who profess "Jesus is Lord," salvation has been relegated to the function of a spiritual "bye" in the contest to get to heaven. In fact, some of our most beloved songs and famous sermons seem to dwell on our "mansion in the sky" or our "home in glory." Accordingly, we sit with our spiritual suitcases packed awaiting our transport from "this old evil world."

Generations of subscribers to such theological presuppositions have never bothered to consider the fallacy of the illogical and spiritually bereft notion that God would train us for managing a mansion in glory by forcing us to live in poverty here on earth, while at the same time instructing us to pray, "Thy kingdom come . . . on earth as it is in heaven! Of course, the same presuppositions would substantiate the apparent similar belief of many that the biblical prophetic summons to become lenders and not borrowers can be fulfilled despite encumbering ourselves with overriding debt, sabotaging our future by failing to sacrifice in the present, and failing to take advantage of rich opportunities to become entrepreneurs and property owners, rather than being satisfied with day labor and tenancy.

In the pages that follow, my good friend, James Giles acutely and accurately diagnoses the failure of essential purpose within the Body of Christ. Moreover, he prescribes a course of treatment spiritually rich and practically applicable, to render this malaise inoperable against future generations.

The Word of God declares the revelation of the mystery of God's plan and purpose. That is, Christ in you . . . the hope of glory. My friend, your home is not just "in glory." Your home is the glory! Arise, shine, for the light is come. The glory of the Lord is risen . . . upon thee! We must reflect His nature and character. We must exemplify His attitude. Yes, even our physical bodies should reflect the fact that a King lives inside.

James Giles articulately and persuasively presents the case for renewal of integrity, honesty, and boldness within the Body of Christ. In short, he summons those of us who have "put on the whole armor of Christ" to stop running from the fight! Rather, he provides clear direction for development of lifestyles that define the parameters of the battlefield with assurance of victory regardless of the battlefront.

My friend, read on. However, I warn you that what you are about to learn will be destructive to antiquated notions of the past which equate Christianity with passivity. Moreover, it will forever challenge you and, I pray, change you to be more than the conqueror you were destined to be.

Dr. Harold Calvin Ray

Preface

Do you yearn to do something significant with your life? Do you feel you're still a long way from fulfilling your destiny? Do you want your unique giftedness to make an eternal impact on the lives of others? Like all too many of us, you may lack vision for your life. Perhaps you're mired in mediocrity, chained to a painful past, or unaware that tremendous potential lies within you. But with God, all of that can change.

The Creator has stamped His image upon you. God has given you talents, skills, and the ability to create. You have a special destiny to fulfill, and God Himself wants to see you realize your potential.

You can do it! How? By yielding yourself to the One who uniquely created you, knows your aspirations and dreams, and understands how to get you there. God longs to be involved in every area of our lives. If we submit ourselves wholeheartedly to God, He offers us an edge in living. Health, prosperity, and blessing flow into our lives. We can strive for excellence and experience His abundant favor. I call this the God Factor, which results from knowing the Creator of the Universe.

When you personally know the Creator, you have the potential to tap into your God-given genius. In the chapters that follow, you'll learn how to make this happen in your life.

Chapter 1

Activating the God Factor

Did you know that by the year 2000, knowledge will double every 18 months? It presently doubles every five years. More knowledge has been produced in the past 30 years than in the previous 5,000 years. Scientists finish 7,000 new research papers each day. Americans sift through over 50,000 advertisements annually. The 50,000 books and 10,000 periodicals that are published each year in the United States give even the most avid reader staggering choices.

In their book, Crystal Globe, Certon and Davies write, "Useful, job-oriented knowledge is becoming increasingly perishable. The half-life of an engineer's professional information today is five years; in ten years, 90 percent of what he knows will be available on computer, while he will be expected to learn new techniques and skills throughout his working life. Eighty five per cent of the information in the U. S. National Institutes of Health computers is upgraded in five years."

Education and illiteracy will look different in the future. Futurist Alvin Toffler has said that the illiterate of the future will not be those who cannot read or write, "but those who cannot learn, unlearn, and relearn." By the year 2000, over 40 percent of the labor force will be involved in collecting, analyzing, synthesizing, structuring, storing, or retrieving information.

Telecommunications technology makes the international information superhighway possible. University of Texas (Austin) professor Frederick Williams defines telecommunications as "in essence, . . . the application of technology to extend the distance over which humans or their intermediaries, such as computers, can communicate."

Developments such as facsimile (FAX), communications satellites, cellular mobile phones, microwave relay, paging, and the ISDN (Integrated Digital Systems Network) are all part of the intelligent network. Both the benefits and potential drawbacks of the proliferation of this technology have been written about extensively and will no doubt receive even more print in the coming decades. Naisbitt and Aburdene suggest in Megatrends 2000 that educated and skilled information workers will garner the highest wages ever during the 1990s.

Your God-Given Genius

God places no premium on ignorance. He laments, "My people are destroyed for lack of knowledge" (Hosea 4:6). Our world is changing so rapidly that we must understand a concept termed "economic alchemy." Articulated by Paul Lane Pilzer, this concept sets forth the notion of ideas as wealth. This is no new idea. God expounded it long ago in His Word.

Pilzer writes, "In the alchemic world, new products create their own demand by changing the way people behave. To put it another way, existing markets are, or very soon will be, dying markets. By the end of the decade, the majority of successful business people will no longer be supplying consumers with products that are simply better at filling existing needs; rather, they will be creating entirely new needs to fill."

I believe our quickly changing world presents us with some great opportunities. Corporate culture is shifting from old structures of pyramid leadership to an inverted pyramid. Business leaders are stimulating minority entrepreneurship.

This is a perfect opportunity for us to rely on the creativity of the Almighty. God's wisdom is not merely for the affairs of the Church. We can manifest divine insight and problem solving on our secular jobs. We must begin to teach the value of knowledge, wisdom, and expertise to those who can greatly benefit from it. Geniuses sit in the pews of churches week after week and have never had their genius tapped and directed.

Polish pianist-composer and patriot Ignace Paderewski (1860-1941) related that a young gushing listener once said to him, "Paderewski, you are truly a genius." He answered, "Yes, madam, I am a genius; but before that I was for many years a drudge." A genius within a drudge! Can you imagine that? What will it take to release the genius within you?

D. Kenneth Winebrenner writes: "Real intelligence is a creative use of knowledge, not merely an accumulation of facts. The slow thinker who can finally come up with an idea of his own is more important to the world than a walking encyclopedia who hasn't learned how to use the information productively."

Genius is being discovered and released all over the world. At this very moment someone is working on an invention that demands their genius to come forth. Because of their curiosity and fascination, something will spring forth that will improve the quality of life for millions — maybe billions — of lives.

Marietta Shaginyan has said, "Man's need to create is just as powerful as his need for food and drink." Ideas swarm all around us. Unfortunately, most of them will be ignored. Stanford Lee has said, "Every day thousands of people bury good ideas because they are afraid to act on them."

Incubate Your Ideas

Christians must meditate upon the ideas God gives them — then gain the knowledge, wisdom, and expertise they need — to bring those ideas to fruition. We are so preoccupied with business and so disparaging of daydreams that our ideas often have no incubator. Daydreaming can be good for you. Most people who let themselves daydream are often refreshed, stimulated, and renewed when they return to what they are doing. Many people work out solutions to problems while they daydream.

Did you know that such things as X rays, penicillin, dynamite, teflon, velcro, and the Dead Sea Scrolls were discovered "by accident"? Serendipity, that marvelous word coined in 1754, is "the faculty for making desirable discoveries by accident." Wallace Hume Carothers discovered nylon by serendipity. Saccharin, cyclamates, and aspertame (NutraSweet) also were discovered this way.

Proverbs 8:12 says, "I wisdom dwell with prudence, and find out knowledge of witty inventions." The Hebrew word for invention means plan, plot, or purpose. Witty is the word sakal (sawkal), meaning intelligent, expert, skillful, prosperous, and successful.

If the church is going to be authentically biblical in its spirituality, it must become an incubator for genius. A major and often neglected aspect of spiritual growth is to help people discover their genius and feed it. The enlarged mind vigorously challenged with new ideas and possibilities is serendipitously fertile. Serendipity stubbornly avoids the inactive mind.

Paul Flory, recipient of the American Chemical Society's highest honor, the Priestly Medal, said:

Significant inventions are not mere accidents. The erroneous view [that they are] is widely held, and it is one that the scientific and technical community, unfortunately, has done little to dispel. Happenstance usually plays a part, to be sure, but there is much more to invention than the particular notion of a bolt out of the blue. Knowledge in depth and in breadth are virtual prerequisites. Unless the mind is thoroughly charged beforehand, the proverbial spark of genius, if it should manifest itself, probably will find nothing to ignite.

"Through desire a man, having separated himself, seeketh and intermeddleth with all wisdom" (Prov. 18:1). Intermeddleth is from the Hebrew word gala (gaw-lah), which means to be obstinate. Desire is delight or satisfaction. A man's desire causes him to draw apart in obstinate pursuit of wisdom. The Bible has shown us how to prepare for serendipity.

You Can Do It!

In Microcosm, an important book by George Gilder, the author states, "The most valuable capital is now the capital of the human mind and spirit. Intellectual capital can transform any physical environment, even a few small, cold, stony islands off the eastern coast of Asia, into a center of production and wealth." This is Gilder's version of economic alchemy.

The uncharted recesses of the human spirit and mind have always been our most valuable resource. The church must participate in the present and the future. We must pray and we must work. As we speak, preach, and teach all over the world, we must challenge believers to be people of critical transformation and meaningful action.

Powerful and ethically relevant shifts are occurring in medicine, law, trade and international finance, education, politics, and religion. The world needs your genius. This act in the drama of history calls upon your faith and courage, your gifts and compassion, your love for God and for all mankind.

Did you know that people all over America have acted on their ideas and are earning millions of dollars right out of their homes? Studies estimate 20.7 million full time home businesses will operate by 1995.

What can you, your friends, and family do to make the world a better place? It may simultaneously generate profit for the kingdom of God and create meaningful employment, training, and growth opportunities. You can do it! Stop paralyzing yourself through fear and small-mindedness. Use this acronym to put fear into perspective. FEAR: False Expectations Appearing Real.

The God Factor is the ingredient that separates you from the masses. You can display it in any calling or vocation, from Christian ministry to athletics or business. Acquiring the wisdom, knowledge, and skills that will make you an expert in your particular field builds the muscle of your God Factor. Once activated, it will change you forever.

Once your God Factor has kicked in, you need to ignite it with enthusiasm. The prophet Jeremiah, a man of passion, had a fire shut up in his bones. Jesus said that the zeal He felt toward His Father's house consumed Him. B. C. Forbes said, "Enthusiasm is the all-essential human jet propellant. It is the driving force which elevates men to miracle workers. It begets boldness, courage; kindles confidence; overcomes doubts. It creates endless energy, the source of all accomplishment."

Michael Pritchard wrote, "Fear is that little dark room where negatives are developed." Fear and faith are opposites. Rid yourself of fear and all you have to lose are boredom, frustration, anxiety, unfulfillment, lack of challenge and adventure, and the very fear itself. Choose faith and allow God to use you in this hour. Activate your God Factor and move out.

Chapter 2

You Can Do Exploits!

Did you know you can have an intimate relationship with the God of heaven and earth? Not only is such a relationship possible, but absolutely necessary if you are going to meet the challenges that confront mankind at this critical juncture in history.

Daniel 11:32 says, "but the people that do know their God shall be strong, and do exploits." Webster's Encyclopedic Unabridged Dictionary of the English Language defines an "exploit" as "a striking or notable deed; spirited or heroic act; accomplishment; achievement." God desires to use you in a most awesome, powerful way. That will only happen, however, as you grow in your knowledge of God.

Strong's Exhaustive Concordance of the Bible tells us "know," which comes from the Hebrew word yada (yaw-dah), means to know by observation, care, recognition, or instruction. Yada also means to be diligent to discover or discern; to have understanding; a familiar friend; kinsfolk; kinsman; to be famous; a man of skill; to be sure.

Knowing God means more than merely going to church. The Father wants to be studied and known in depth. Daniel told us that when we really know God, we will be a transformed people — a people destined to do great things.

"For we are his workmanship, created in Jesus Christ unto good works, which God hath before ordained that we should walk in them" (Ephesians 2:10).

"Workmanship" in this verse comes from the Greek word poiema, from poieo. Poiema literally means a thing that is made, crafted, or constructed. Our English word poem comes from poiema. One fascinating meaning is to be raised up and purged to accomplish purpose.

God is not interested in vain worship and shallow ceremony. Neither is He interested in legalistic holier than thouism. God yearns for a people who understand that our times beckon us to eschew the average and mock the mediocre. God wants a people who will shake nations, kingdoms, and cities for Him — a people who think, speak, pray, give, and live in a way that will impact generations.

The Bible is full of the deeds of men and women who knew God. Their exploits often preserved the Israelites, a race called to worship and enter into covenant with the God of heaven and earth. Let's look at a few examples of those who knew God and performed exploits. As we study their lives, we can glean several principles to challenge us to new heights of greatness.

Don't Be Greedy

God created Adam, the first man, on the continent of Africa. He knew the voice of God and walked with Him in the cool of the garden. Adam knew God in a way that no man would know Him until Jesus the Son of God came in the flesh. That's quite a statement, given the relationship of many Old Testament saints.

Adam's knowledge of God commissioned him to be the father of the human race and to oversee God's entire investment portfolio with its incalculable net worth. Adam, however, was instructed not to touch one investment — which was God's perogative as the Creator. Having almost everything was not good enough for Adam — he wanted everything, and that damaged his relationship with God.

In the same way today, discontentment and greed will strain your relationship with God.

God put wealth in the earth to bless us and to facilitate our God-given creative powers. God also put wealth in the earth to eliminate poverty and all its deleterious consequences. Poverty is not a natural state of existence. God's intent for man can be seen by the abundant provision He gave to Adam.

When the Israelites had been victorious in battle, God often instructed them to plunder the defeated nations of their wealth to finance God's opulent building projects, to provide for His priests, and to improve the general quality of life for all His people.

How many pastors languish in despair because the vision in their hearts exceeds the offering in the plate? How many would-be scholars, medical and law students, and entrepreneurs depend upon the vicissitudes of government to permit the fulfillment of their divine dreams and purposes? The church of the living God should be able to finance the education of its own. I believe that God wants His people wealthy — not simply to live lavish, undisciplined lifestyles, but so that God's agenda will not be hampered by the lack of sufficient finances.

See the Big Picture

We know that greed and disobedience eventually caused Adam to be expelled from the garden, but God's plan for mankind didn't grind to a halt. Later Noah, a "preacher of righteousness" (2 Peter 2:5), came on the scene. He knew God and was charged with bringing a righteous remnant from his own loins to God. What Adam failed to accomplish, Noah was called upon to do.

Can you imagine the Lord God visiting you and saying, "My human race is messed up. They have fallen short of My lofty purposes for them. I have watched you. You are a righteous man, and if you don't mind I'd like to use you, your wife, your sons, and their wives . . ."

And God saw that the wickedness of man was great in the earth, and that every imagination of the thoughts of his heart was only evil continually. And it repented the Lord that he had made man on the earth, and it grieved him at his heart. And the Lord said, I will destroy man whom I have created from the face of the earth, both man, and beast, and the creeping thing, and the fowls of the air; for it repenteth me that I have made them. But Noah found grace in the eyes of the Lord (Genesis 6:5-8).

God spoke to Noah: "But with thee will I establish my covenant; and thou shalt come into the ark, thou, and thy sons, and thy wife, and thy sons' wives with thee" (Genesis 6:18). I don't know about you, but being confined to a floating zoo for several months is not my idea of the glory cloud. Noah, however, knew that this was necessary to produce a new redeemed race.

The ark was not a cruise ship, and Noah didn't have the luxury of taking a vacation. The animals had to be fed. His wife and three daughters-in-law needed his attention. If his sons were newlyweds, Noah probably had difficulty getting them to help with the chores. Cleaning up after all those animals was anything but a promising, upwardly mobile position.

Nevertheless, Noah saw the big picture. That's what visionaries do. Genesis 7:5 says, "And Noah did according unto all that the Lord commanded him.... and Noah only remained alive, and they that were with him in the ark.... And God remembered Noah . . ." (Genesis 7:5,23; 8:1). What a testimony! God promised to never again curse the ground for man's sake, thus implementing the perpetual reality of seedtime and harvest.

We will never exhaust the testimonies of all those who have done exploits for God. Men and women who knew God have overcome the impossible, been victorious in the face of defeat, and left a legacy to tell about it. Let's look at a few more individuals. Remember, there is nothing common or mundane about the person who knows God.

St. Augustine, the remarkable African theologian, said, "God is not greater if you reverence Him, but you are greater if you serve Him."

Holding on to Hope

Moses, a man of great exploits, was abandoned at birth and raised by a single parent. Despite those humble beginnings, God placed Moses in the center of Pharaoh's court. There he received the knowledge and training to one day lead his people, an amalgamation of Israelites and Egypto-Asiatics, out of Egypt and into freedom. God took a ragtag bunch of former slaves and turned them into the richest, mightiest nation on the earth. The Israelites knew their God.

In God you can go from nobody to somebody, from poor to rich, from being a loser to being a champion. I believe that everyone wants to be a champion. Everyone dreams of accomplishing something noteworthy and helping others to fulfill their own dreams and visions.

Have you ever heard people fantasize about what they would do if they won the lottery? They almost always mention some kind deed for a friend or a loved one. Many people, however, including committed Christians, do not have enough faith in God or in themselves to believe that their dreams can come true.

Proverbs 13:12 says, "Hope deferred maketh the heart sick: but when the desire cometh, it is a tree of life." Hope, in this verse, means expectation. Those who know God should burst with expectation over the great things about to happen in their lives. When this hope is deferred, you often grow discouraged. The Hebrew word for "deferred" is mashak (maw-shak), which literally means to delay, to draw or stretch out, to prolong.

To prolong the hope that God's expectation will be fulfilled can make you heartsick. The heart is the mind, or the seat of reflection and volition. The Hebrew word for sickness is chalah (khaw-law), which means to be rubbed or worn; to be weak or afflicted; to be sorry, wounded, or diseased. The Bible repeatedly shows us the relationship between mental and physical health. Pursuing your God-given dream and expectation has a marked healing effect, particularly on your mind.

Many of us start out where Moses did, and we tend to predict our future based upon our present or past. We face mountains too high to climb and rivers too wide to cross with faith too low to shimmy under. If this describes you, congratulations! You are right where God has found many of His champions. Overwhelming circumstances motivate many people to begin their pursuit of God. As we seek Him, God delights in revealing His character and nature to us. God really wants us to know Him:

[That you may really come] to know — practically, through experience for yourselves — the love of Christ, which far surpasses mere knowledge (without experience); that you may be filled (through all your being) unto all the fullness of God — [that is] may have the richest measure of the divine Presence, and become a body wholly filled and flooded with God Himself!

Now to Him Who, by (in consequence of) the [action of His] power that is at work within us, is able to [carry out His purpose and] do superabundantly, far over and above all that we [dare] ask or think — infinitely beyond our highest prayers, desires, thoughts, hopes, or dreams — to Him be glory in the church and in Christ Jesus throughout all generations, for ever and ever. Amen — so be it (Ephesians 3:19-21, Amplified).

As you study those verses and meditate upon the truth they contain, the truth will set you free. Knowing God is to be filled and flooded with Him. He promises us the richest measure of His presence. God is able, as a consequence of His power, to do super abundantly above what we can desire! The greatest thing in the world that you or I may desire does not even begin to test, much less exhaust, God's power. The issue is not what God can or cannot do; it is what we will ask for, work for, and expect.

A Few Hours of Greatness

God is great and greatly to be praised. Scripture tells us that God will have glory throughout the ages. Maybe you think the only way to glorify God is to look somber and holy, to shout and cry a little bit, memorize as many Bible verses as possible, and try to love your neighbor. All those are good, but let me ask you a question: What are you doing with the gifts, skills, and talents that God has given you?

You may attend church faithfully, and you certainly should, but if God is calling you into law, medicine, architecture, ministry, teaching, writing, academia, or any other area, and you are doing nothing, you are in rebellion. James 4:17 says, "Therefore to him that knoweth to do good, and doeth it not, to him it is sin."

Someone once said, "Great men have but a few hours to be great." Like the rest of us, great men must dress, bathe, and eat; they must visit the dentist, doctor, and barber and confer with their wives about domestic matters. Great men, however, have the ability to decide what is important and then focus their attention on that.

Let's look at two of Israel's judges who knew what to do in "the few hours" God gave them.

God has a tendency to consider His people far more powerful and valuable than they themselves may realize. Take Gideon, for instance. Gideon's name actually means warrior, or one who cuts down or destroys. Apparently, when Gideon's parents named him, they had a special destiny in mind. Gideon, however, doubted that he had any significance or purpose. He was not even sure that God was with His people.

And the angel of the Lord appeared unto him, and said unto him, The Lord is with thee, thou mighty man of valour. And Gideon said unto him, Oh my Lord, if the Lord be with us, why then is all this befallen us? and where be all his miracles which our fathers told us of, saying, Did not the Lord bring us up from Egypt? but now the Lord hath forsaken us, and delivered us into the hands of the Midianites (Judges 6:12,13).

After testing God several times, Gideon gained the reassurance he needed to lead Israel into battle. He built an altar, saw God whittle thousands of troops down to a mere band of 300, and defeated the enemies of God. Those who know their God shall be strong and do exploits.

Overcoming Despair

How can we talk about strength and not mention Samson? Samson had the special challenge of God upon him from his mother's womb. Before this mighty man came into the world, however, his father and mother struggled with their inability to conceive.

And the children of Israel did evil again in the sight of the Lord; and the Lord delivered them into the hands of the Philistines forty years. And there was a certain man of Zorah, of the family of the Danites, whose name was Manoah; and his wife was barren, and bare not.

And the angel of the Lord appeared unto the woman, and said unto her, Behold now, thou art barren, and barest not: but thou shalt conceive, and bear a son. Now therefore beware, I pray thee, and drink not wine nor strong drink, and eat not any unclean thing: For, lo, thou shalt conceive, and bear a son; and no [razor] shall come on his head: for the child shall be a Nazarite unto God from the womb: and he shall begin to deliver Israel out of the hand of the Philistines (Judges 13:1-5).

When you are pregnant with a vision from God, you will discipline yourself and sacrifice just like Manoah's wife. She did not touch alcohol or eat the wrong kinds of food because she carried within her the deliverance of Israel. Years of barrenness brought public shame upon her and her husband. Her childlessness probably provoked some domestic disputes and certainly did not help her self-esteem.

Are you facing a predicament similar to Manoah's wife? Perhaps your barrenness or lack of accomplishment brings you public embarrassment and private despair. The same God who remembered Manoah's wife wants you to know Him. No matter how barren you feel, you have God-given potential for greatness.

Maybe you are like Manoah. You need to keep on sowing the seed of your desire by faith. Do not look to circumstances. "He that observeth the wind shall not sow; and he that regardeth the clouds shall not reap.... In the morning sow thy seed, and in the evening withhold not thy hand: for thou knowest not whether shall prosper, either this or that, or whether they both shall be alike good" (Eccl. 11:4,6).

Even though his wife was barren, Manoah continued to make love to her. He continued to sow seed in hope of someday having a son. God is a God of fruitfulness, and He gives this promise to those who seek to know Him: "For if these things be in you, and abound, they make you that ye shall neither be barren nor unfruitful in the knowledge of our Lord Jesus Christ" (2 Peter 1:8).

Prepare for Greatness

David, Israel's king and sweet singer of songs, certainly had inauspicious beginnings. David's family thought so highly of him that when the prophet Samuel came to their home looking for candidates for kingship, David was not even included. What a case of overlooked potential. His parents probably did love David, but love is one thing and kingship is another. Let's look at his call to the throne.

> *And the Lord said unto Samuel, How long wilt thou mourn for Saul, seeing I have rejected him from reigning over Israel? fill thine horn with oil, and go, I will send thee to Jesse the Bethlehemite: for I have provided me a king among his sons.... And it came to pass, when they were come, that he looked on Eliab, and said, Surely the Lord's anointed is before him. But the Lord said unto Samuel, Look not on his countenance, or on the height of his stature; because I have refused him: for the Lord seeth not as man seeth; for man looketh on the outward appearance, but the Lord looketh on the heart.... And Samuel said unto Jesse, Are here all thy children? And he said, There remaineth yet the youngest, and, behold, he keepeth the sheep. And Samuel said unto Jesse, Send and fetch him: for we will not sit down till he come hither. And he sent, and brought him in. Now he was ruddy, and withal of a beautiful countenance, and goodly to look to. And the Lord said, Arise, anoint him: for this is he. Then Samuel took the horn of oil, and anointed him in the midst of his brethren: and the Spirit of the Lord came upon David from that day forward. So Samuel rose up, and went to Ramah (1 Samuel 16:1,6,7,11-13).*

I'm glad the Bible says that the Spirit of the Lord came upon David "from that day forward." The Holy Spirit still anoints today "from that day forward." God commissions us to look toward the future, not the past. One of the biggest hindrances to knowing God is being shackled to the past.

Even though the prophet Samuel had anointed him to rule the nation, David made a pact to serve the reigning King Saul. David — whose name means a love-token, lover, friend, or beloved — lived up to those admirable character qualities. He also had developed skill in several areas before entering the king's service.

But the Spirit of the Lord departed from Saul, and an evil spirit from the Lord troubled him. And Saul's servants said unto him, Behold now, an evil spirit from God troubleth thee. Let our lord now command thy servants, which are before thee, to seek out a man, who is a cunning player on an harp: and it shall come to pass, when the evil spirit from God is upon thee, that he shall play with his hand, and thou shalt be well. And Saul said unto his servants, Provide me now a man that can play well, and bring him to me. Then answered one of the servants, and said, Behold I have seen a son of Jesse the Bethlehemite, that is cunning in playing, and a mighty valiant man, and a man of war, and prudent in matters, and a comely person, and the Lord is with him (1 Samuel 16:14-18).

This does not sound like a man who had accepted mediocrity. Shepherding sheep was an important responsibility for an agricultural and pastoral people, but David had more lofty aspirations.

I am not promoting an attitude that says, "God, I am so great, so skilled, and so talented that You must use me." That distasteful arrogance is totally unacceptable to God. But we also must not grovel in sloth, self-pity, and false spirituality, saying, "If God wants to use me, He will. If He doesn't, He won't. I'll be content as long as I can make heaven my home."

Before entering the king's service, David must have been doing something besides tending sheep. David mastered a musical instrument, studied the wisdom of the fathers, and learned the science of war. How much of an investment do you have in yourself? How prepared are you to do great exploits for God? Someone once said that if you are unprepared when your greatest opportunity comes, it will only make a fool of you.

Cheering Great Skill

Scripture describes David as "cunning" on his instrument. The Hebrew word for cunning is the same word yada (yaw-dah), as in knowing God. As David studied the harp by observation, care, and instruction, he became the friend and kinsman of that instrument. This shepherd became a man of such great skill that when the king needed a harpist, David's reputation had preceded him. He knew this truth: "Do you see a man skilled in his work? He will serve before kings; he will not serve before obscure men" (Prov. 22:29, NIV).

Strong's Concordance reveals that word skill comes from the same word, you guessed it, yadah (yaw-daw). Skill is also from another Hebrew word biyn (bene), meaning to separate mentally, to understand; to be eloquent and instructed, to be or have intelligence. Another word for skill is the Hebrew word sakal (saw-kal), which means to be expert, to be prosperous, to have good success, to behave oneself wisely.

We all appreciate and admire skill. That's why we pay to hear a talented musician or purchase our favorite author's works. We applaud high-scoring athletes and read the biographies of our heroes.

Why do we attend little league contests to cheer on the next Bo Jackson, Larry Bird, Ken Griffey, Jr., or Roger Clemens? Why do we encourage our children to watch Debbi Thomas or Christy Yamaguchi? We do it because we love to cheer extraordinary discipline, skill, and greatness.

David defended his nation from the threat of Goliath when the entire Israelite army stood paralyzed with fear. At 13 feet, four inches tall, Goliath towered over the youth. His armor weighed over 300 pounds; his spears weighed 24 pounds each. But David, a man with a mission and a passion, overcame staggering odds to conquer the giant. His victory ignited bravery in an entire nation. The courage and exploits of one man — David — marked the turning point in the Israelites' standoff with the Philistines.

The Greatest Champion Who Ever Lived

A wise man, R. S. Donnell, once wrote, "The man who follows a crowd will never be followed by a crowd." This statement is especially true of the greatest champion to ever live — Jesus Christ Himself. Jesus Christ knew God so well that He could say, "I and my Father are one" (John 10:30). One in the Greek is the word heis (hice), which means abundantly one; one in numeric identity; the whole number one. Jesus Christ said that He and God the Creator were a whole number One. Jesus readily identified with God the Father. In fact, He said, "Anyone who has seen me has seen the Father" (John 14:9, NIV).

Who in history has lived a life of such courage, such conviction, and such faith? Who has spoken so profoundly to human suffering and brokenness? Who has lived such a selfless life and brought such joy and healing to others? Who has performed deeds that have inspired more of the world's art, literature, music, poetry, and drama? Who has carried a deeper and greater love for all mankind?

The only man to ever enjoy His unique oneness with God freely shared it. The only one innocent of missing the mark before God implored the Father to accept the sacrifice. An innocent man's life was exchanged for our sin and shortcomings. The one who was rejected in every way encourages us to learn the way of forgiveness. The one who loved God the most also, in apparent contradiction, loved man the most. The One who "ever liveth to make intercession" (Hebrews 7:25) still prays for us today.

Who is a greater champion? Who is a greater warrior? No one! Jesus promises that the same Holy Spirit, who indwelt and inspired Him to great and mighty exploits, will indwell us and we shall do greater works than His. What an awesome, yet humbling, responsibility He has given to us.

I have heard it said that, "When your shoulders are carrying a load of responsibility, there isn't room for chips." Jesus Christ knew that He had been sent here to fulfill a divine purpose, and He accomplished all His Father's will.

Dr. Myles Munroe said there is more unrealized potential in the graveyard than anywhere else. God the Father did not waste Jesus Christ's life, death, and resurrection so that we could sit around doing nothing except apologizing and making excuses. His power is at work within us. Get busy. Become greatly skilled so that God can use you in the manner He so chooses.

Stand Up and Roar!

Thank God, we have people who know their God and are doing exploits in many areas. Dr. Benjamin Carson, Johns Hopkins' Director of Pediatric Neurosurgery, came from the ghettos of Detroit and could barely read by the time he was in fifth grade. Thanks to a godly, praying mother — who believed in him and challenged him to be the best — and to some special teachers, who recognized his potential, Dr. Carson is one of the foremost neurosurgeons in America today.

How could anyone forget the courage of baseball pitcher Dave Dravecki who wrestled with career-ending cancer and told the world of his faith in God? He met the challenges in his life and became a hero.

Dr. Frederic K. C. Price built one of the largest churches in America by teaching people to know their God and believe Him for all that He promises. Brother Jawanza Kunjufu, a man of God and a teacher, has restored hope to downtrodden people. We will never forget the Rev. Dr. Martin Luther King who knew his God and challenged the soul of a nation by exhorting us to be truly human and truly humane. Florence Griffith Joyner won our hearts at the Olympic Games in Seoul, Korea with her flashy costumes, unparalleled athletic excellence, and her radiant beauty and humility. These men and women, and many others, challenge us to aspire to excellence.

I would like to introduce you to a champion you may have never met before — someone special and unique with precious gifts and a marvelous destiny. Someone extra special to the God of all creation.

That someone is you! Yes, you! Today can be the beginning of a bold new adventure in living for you. If you will seize the day and determine to know the God who fills men and women with limitless, inexhaustible power, you can positively impact your family, your community, your nation, and your world.

Proverbs 28:1 says, "the righteous are bold as a lion." Stand up today and roar! Proclaim that you will no longer accept defeat, succumb to sloth, or wallow in self-pity. Proclaim that from this day forward, as the Holy Spirit comes upon you afresh, you are a champion, a strong warrior, and a doer of exploits!

Chapter 3

Big Steps to a Bright Future

Every book I've ever read on success and achievement agrees that a positive self image is one of the fundamental building blocks for successful living. Christians, however, hold a variety of opinions as to whether or not self-image is important. Self-image must be important because God informs us in the Bible that we are made in His image. What a profound truth: to be made in the image of God.

While contemporary literature uses the terms self-esteem, self-image, and self-concept interchangeably, for our purposes, we will use self-esteem.

Dr. Robert Schuller of the Crystal Cathedral and the "Hour of Power" telecast has written many helpful books attempting to pull people from the mire of low self-esteem. He defines self-esteem as "the human hunger for the divine dignity that God intended to be our emotional birthright as children created in his image." *Webster's New World Dictionary* defines dignity "as the quality of being worthy of esteem or honor; worthiness."

You may ask, "If God intends us to have divine dignity and emotional health, why do most people experience such emotional turmoil and lack of fulfillment?" Dr. Schuller writes, "I contend that this unfulfilled need for self-esteem underlies every human act, both negative and positive. Every analysis of social or personal sins must recognize that the core of all sinful or unsocial behavior is a conscious or subconscious attempt to feed the person's need for self-esteem." Whether or not you agree with Dr. Schuller's conclusion, the notion is very plausible and bears serious reflection.

Scripture says, "For as he thinketh in his heart, so is he" (Prov. 23:7). You and I continually carry around with us a picture of ourselves. We constantly think about who we are, how we look, what we have or haven't done, and what relationships we have or have not built. At any moment, our self-image propels us toward great accomplishment or hurls us toward defeat. We even think with our self-image. The way we see ourselves largely influences the decisions we make on a daily basis.

What Does God Think?

Our self-image greatly affects us, but is it always reliable? Our opinions, feelings, and conclusions about life aren't always true. We need to turn to a more trustworthy gauge of our worth. What does God think about us? This passage of Scripture provides some insight.

What is man, that thou art mindful of him? and the son of man, that thou visitest him? For thou hast made him a little lower than the angels, and hast crowned him with glory and honour. Thou madest him to have dominion over the works of thy hands; thou hast put all things under his feet (Psalm 8:4-6).

Let's study some of the words in this passage. First, God is mindful of man. Mindful is the Hebrew word *zakar* (zaw-kar), meaning to mark or to think well on; to keep in remembrance. How it would bolster the self-esteem of men, women, and children everywhere to know that the God who created the wondrous peaks of the Cascade Mountains, the tropical splendor of the Hawaiian Islands, and the depth and beauty of the world's oceans cares about them!

God loves you and me with passion — with the depth of His very being — which the Bible tells us is love. Many churches and preachers have represented God as an angry old man who gets some sort of sinister pleasure from punishing people for their failures and shortcomings. No way. The great news is that God loves us so much that He sent His only Son to provide the forgiveness and power we need to live awesome, inspired lives.

Next, God promises to visit man. Visitest is the Hebrew word *paqad* (paw-kad), meaning to oversee; to appoint by mandate; to care for. God is not unlike any other doting parent. He wants His children to succeed. This is a profound truth. God so desires His children to succeed that He appoints you and me to a marvelous destiny. If we cooperate with Him, He oversees this destiny.

What comes to mind when you think of angels? You may think of powerful beings who transcend time and space. Perhaps you think of beautiful creatures who delight in singing praises to the Creator and assisting Him with blessing mankind.

Although our images of angels differ, most of us would agree that they are pretty awesome. Psalm 8:5 says that we are made "a little lower than the angels." Lower literally means that we are in a very small matter lacking all of what the angels have. What feats of God-glorifying wonder would you and I attempt if we really understood this truth? The days of sitting around, making excuses, and feeling sorry for ourselves would be over.

Psalm 8 tells us that God has "crowned us with glory and honour." Crowned is the word *atar* (aw-tar), which means to encircle for protection. Glory carries incredible meaning. The Hebrew word is *kabod* (kaw-bode), meaning weight, splendor, or copiousness. The word also means rich, honorable, very great.

Honor is from a Hebrew word that literally means magnificence, ornamentation, and splendor. The word also means to be highly favored, beautiful, excellent, goodly, and glorious. Why should we grovel in the pain of low self-esteem when God says He has encircled us with magnificence and splendor?

Wherever you are right now, get up and go to the closest mirror. Look at yourself and say, "Behold, a wondrous creation of God." Say out loud, "God has encircled me with magnificence. He has ornamented me with splendor. I was never created to grovel in shame and mediocrity. I was created to soar majestically in the loftiest clouds, to stand on the summit of great mountain peaks."

Say it, sing it, shout it! Enjoy a good, soul-stirring laugh, or cry a little if you need to. It's perfectly all right! You'll feel like a new person and that, my friend, is a worthy indulgence.

A Fresh Start

Because our self-esteem is based largely upon memories, the renewal of the mind contributes greatly to our journey toward godly self-esteem. Layers of toxic memories and negative self-talk have to be replaced with the truths of God's Word. Some people develop lifestyles of depression, defeat, failure, fatigue, and various addictive behaviors. Many persons in these predicaments understandably look for someone to blame, finding it too painful to accept responsibility for the mess their lives have become. Even if someone else is to blame, there is one very important fact to remember: As long as you or I refuse to take responsibility for changing our own lives, no change will occur.

If anyone had a past that could haunt him, it was the apostle Paul. His contemporaries could have accused him of being a religious bigot, murderer, and elitist Pharisee — and they would have been right. But God gave him a fresh start, and Paul made the most of it. Do you remember his attitude about the past?

Brethren, I count not myself to have apprehended: but this one thing I do, forgetting those things which are behind, and reaching forth unto those things which are before, I press toward the mark for the prize of the high calling of God in Christ Jesus (Phil. 3:13,14).

Paul set a goal not only of forgetting his past but of reaching forward and shaping his future. When you are shackled to the past, you cannot shape the future. Paul used urgent language to describe his pursuit of the future. He said, "I press toward the mark." The word "press" comes from the Greek word *dioko* (dee-o-ko), which means to serve fearfully. In effect, Paul tells us that the believer must be afraid not to pursue the future.

We must live in fear of *not* fulfilling our destiny. This is not legalism; it is biblical truth. God did not redeem and fill us with the Holy Spirit so that we could sit around waiting for Christ to return.

Do not delay another moment. A whole new life of peace, joy, and strength awaits those of us who will accept responsibility for the future.

Eight Steps to a Bright Future

Here are some steps to take to make your future a bright one:

1. *Ask yourself if you are pleased with the quality of your life.* This includes your sense of personal accomplishment or lack of the same. It also includes the quality of your personal and professional relationships, finances, as well as your spiritual, emotional, and physical health.

2. *Write down* all the things you are not satisfied with along with the reasons for your dissatisfaction.

3. *Accept responsibility for change!* You are only stuck if you choose to be. One of the greatest powers that God has given us is the power to choose.

4. *Set new goals* for growth and change in four areas of life.

    a. Personal development goals

    b. Professional/business/financial goals

    c. Joy/adventure goals

    d. Charitable, "what-will-I-give-back" goals

Goals are the road map to your future. Attempting to live a prosperous and fulfilled life without goals is like traveling cross-country without a road map. Earl Nightingale said, "To achieve happiness, we should make certain that we are never without an important goal." Perhaps you believe that goal setting is unspiritual and that whatever God truly wants you to have will simply happen. Wrong. When you write down your goals, you become serious about the planning process.

5. *Be determined.* Perseverance will keep you from giving up.

6. *Take action.* Dreams alone will get you nowhere. Someone has said, "Doers get to the top of the oak tree by climbing it. Dreamers sit on an acorn." Carl Bowen exhorts us with these words: "The world is looking for the man who can do something, not for the man who can explain why he did not do it."

7. *Become a constant learner.* Study the Bible and other books on goal setting, human behavior, self-esteem, etc. Atwood H. Townsend cautions us, "No matter how busy you may think you are, you must find time for reading, or surrender yourself to self-chosen ignorance."

8. *Commit your venture to prayer.* God's Word explains how: "Roll your works upon the Lord —commit and trust them wholly to Him; [He will cause your thoughts to become agreeable to His will, and] so shall your plans be established and succeed" (Prov. 16:3, Amplified).

Embarking upon this process will begin to give focus and clarity to your life. Your negative past will fight against your positive, faith filled future, but the future is worth the fight. Remember, all true self-esteem must emanate from God. The Bible declares, "If God be for us, who can be against us?" (Romans 8:31).

William A. Ward agrees. He said, "God wants us to be victors, not victims; to grow, not grovel; to soar, not sink; to overcome, not to be overwhelmed."

Don't Blame Your Family

In matters of self-esteem, we tend to live up or down to other people's expectations. Our self-image often consists of the way we feel others perceive us. Swiss psychiatrist Paul Tournier made a distinction between the person and the personage: the person being what we really are; the personage being that public representation of a pseudo-self or image.

In his book, *The Meaning of Persons*, Dr. Tournier writes, "We are the slaves of the personage which we have invented for ourselves or which has been imposed on us by others." He further states, "If one thoughtlessly calls a child a liar, one makes him a liar, in spite of all his aspirations toward honesty. He is still at the age when the frontier between myth and reality is imprecise. People tell him fairy-stories; if he invents stories, he tells them as if they had really happened and finds himself called a liar. Call a child stupid, and you make him stupid, incapable of showing what he has it in him to do.... The power of suggestion exercised by the labels we were given is considerable."

Dr. Maurice E. Wagner writes, "It is probably accurate to assume that the unconscious mind never forgets an experience. The mind may not have the capacity for immediate recall, but the memory is still there. With a different context of associations, we are surprised by how clearly we can recall incidents we thought we had completely forgotten." Remember, self-esteem is composed largely of memories.

One of our great dilemmas results from realizing our worth before God and simultaneously struggling to reach our potential in life. Though we are created by God, we are born into basic social systems called families. In many cases these families consist of battered and bruised parents or primary caregivers. Because of the nonresolution of their own life challenges, they are unable to provide us with the spiritual and emotional environment that would allow us to grow up with healthy self-esteem.

You and I should not be ashamed of this reality, particularly since it is the experience of most Americans. Families — instead of being havens of security, love, trust, and value — often propagate generations of negative family secrets and shame-based parents. In his book, *The Family*, John Bradshaw writes, "Parenting forms children's core belief about themselves. Nothing could be more important. Children are any culture's greatest natural resource. The future of the world depends on our children's conceptions of themselves. All their choices depend on their view of themselves." Mr. Bradshaw also defines shame for us:

> *Depression, alienation, self-doubt, isolating loneliness, paranoia and schizoid phenomena, compulsive disorders, splitting of the self, perfectionism, a deep sense of inferiority, inadequacy or failure, the so-called borderline conditions and disorders of narcissism, all result from shame. Shame is a kind of soul murder. Once shame is internalized, it is characterized by a kind of psychic numbness, which becomes the foundation for a kind of death in life. Forged in the matrix of our source relationships, shame conditions every other relationship in our lives. Shame is a total non-self acceptance.*

Christian families are not exempt from this debilitating shame. We often mask it carefully because we are ashamed and fear being rejected if we reveal our pain. Believing that Christians should not experience this sort of pain further complicates this issue. Many people often then move into a psychotic form of denial and mask their reality with empty religious slogans and contrived smiles.

Dr. Susan Forward, in her book, *Toxic Parents*, writes, "Like a chemical toxin, the emotional damage inflicted by these parents spreads throughout a child's being, and as the child grows, so does the pain." What better word than toxic to describe parents who inflict ongoing trauma, abuse, and denigration on their children, and, in most cases, continue to do so even after their children are grown?

All this talk about shame-based, dysfunctional families does not allow us to blame our parents for our lives. Our goal is not fault-finding but healing.

The Bible tells us that Joseph certainly came from a shame- and rage-based family. If anyone had painful childhood memories, Joseph did. Yet his deep-rooted love for his family enabled him to forgive, and God used his willingness to forgive to heal the entire family. What a sight it must have been to see the patriarch Jacob, his sons, and grandsons reconciling tearfully in the palace.

If we realize our parents are working with their own sense of deficiency, it saves us the wasted energy of placing blame.

Overcoming Anger

As a pastor, I often talk with young men who are angry with their fathers. Men who abandon their families contribute to the increasing number of female headed, single parent households — and the emotional turmoil of the next generation. Many young men reach their teen, young adult, and adult years having never seen or spoken with their fathers. Their emotions vary from repressed anger to overt rage and blatant denial of the father's existence.

One such angry, young man whom I'll call Paul came to my office. Involved in many self-destructive behaviors, he abused alcohol and lived as close to the edge as possible. At the same time, he was bright, articulate, and aspired to be a medical doctor. An avid reader, he was quite conversant on many other issues as well. What internal turmoil to aspire to greatness and, at the same time, be caught in a web of self-destructive behaviors over which one feels powerless.

I, too, once carried a seething rage inside me. I was angry at the world, at my father and mother, my grandparents, at former girlfriends, and almost anyone else. I didn't even understand my own rage. Try as I might, it just seemed impossible to break free from my anger. People whose opinions mattered the most gave up on me, which just made things worse. Suicide entered my mind several times. Why don't you just end it, man? Life's too tough! You'll never get it together, I thought.

No one understood my pain except for my aunt — Joan Capdeville Cook. Aunt Jo, as she is affectionately known, a five-foot, one-inch Louisiana fireball, kept telling me, "Baby, you are gonna be all right. You are smart, and someday you are gonna be somebody great." She kept telling me this when I did not believe it myself. When I was using drugs and alcohol, she kept saying the same thing. When I dropped out of college and lost my job, she still encouraged me. Even today she continues to bless my life. Everyone needs an Aunt Jo to love and encourage them through the difficult periods of life.

As we learn the ways of God and commit ourselves to personal growth, we receive God's power to forgive and the prospect of seeing our families healed. As children we may hold in our hands the release of our parents to their God-given dignity. Maybe your father and mother are ashamed of their failings as parents. Don't remind them what a terrible job they did and how they are responsible for your present circumstances. Forgive your parents. Encourage them to move on with their lives. Try to understand them better and pray for them regularly.

Pursuing Plans for the Future

Despite my upbringing and trials, God has blessed my life. I am fulfilling my dream of writing and speaking to help the discouraged and hopeless. I haven't touched drugs, cigarettes, or painkillers since 1980. Unfortunately, my friend Paul never realized his dream. At the age of 24, while under the influence of alcohol, Paul had a terrible automobile accident that claimed his life. I remain deeply affected by his death.

Like Paul, many people harbor chronic pain without even understanding its source. Old and young people alike lack a compelling, healing dream to propel them through life. In many cases they have given up. People inside and outside the church need to know that — in spite of the pain and dysfunction of their pasts — God still loves them. They can get healed and move beyond the past.

Your value in the sight of God has nothing to do with your family, friends, or any person. You are special to God because He made you in His image and after His likeness.

In his book, *Born To Win*, Lewis Timberlake writes, "God didn't create you, engineer you for success, and then let you dream dreams of achievement in order to taunt you. You have to choose less than God's best for you not to be the man or woman you want to be and were created to be. God gave you talents and abilities to use, not to waste." Sometimes we have to peel away negative layers to get to that person God intends for us to be.

We don't need to prove our spirituality by living in deprivation and calling it "suffering for the Lord." God wants us to be emotionally healthy with our material needs met. Psalm 35:27 says, "Let them shout for joy, and be glad, that favour my righteous cause: yea, let them say continually, Let the Lord be magnified, which hath pleasure in the prosperity of his servant."

God wants us to prosper. After all, He is a parent. Who can believe that God enjoys punishing His children all the time?

When Jeremiah and his beloved nation experienced despair, God sent a comforting word. He said to the ailing prophet, "'For I know the plans I have for you,' declares the Lord, 'plans to prosper you and not to harm you, plans to give you hope and a future'" (Jer. 29:11, NIV).

Ben Nathan offers these words by which to live: "Do not judge the future by the past. In the past may be wisdom, but in the future is life and the miracles of living which know no end. The past has experiences, but the future has surprises. The past produces memory, but the future produces expectation and hope.... The past is closed, but the future is open."

Steps to Healthy Self-Esteem

To begin building positive self-esteem, I encourage you to work through the following process. You may not be able to implement all these steps at once, but start somewhere and start today.

1. *Decide today to live for the future*, not the past. Use the past as a springboard, not as a sofa.

2. *Write down* the things you like and do not like about yourself. Include your appearance, performance, and status.

3. *Vividly imagine the future you desire.*

4. *Accept God's love* not only for yourself but for those loved ones you previously may have held responsible for your life.

5. *Decide to passionately pursue greatness.* Someone has said, "No rule for success will work, if you don't."

6. *Make new positive friends.* Henry Ford said, "My best friend is the one who brings out the best in me."

7. *Develop a strategic plan for self-renovation.*

8. *Practice patience.* Emerson said, "A man is a hero, not because he is braver than anyone else, but because he is brave for ten minutes longer."

9. *Become a giver.* Duane Hulse said, "We make a living by what we get; we make a life by what we give." Karl Menninger agreed. He said, "Money is a good criterion of a person's mental health. Generous people are rarely mentally ill people."

If you need affirmation, give it. We all need forgiveness, so give that also. Help others to attain their goals. Encourage them when they are about to give up. This will improve the quality of your life. People suffering from low self-esteem can rarely be found helping others.

10. *Set high standards for yourself.* Ronald Osborn offers this advice: "Undertake something that is difficult; it will do you good. Unless you try to do something beyond what you have already mastered, you will never grow."

11. *Accept others where they are,* but help them to dream and set goals for a better future.

Chapter 4

How to Develop Your God-Given Creativity

The development of a healthy self-image is not an end in itself. Being made in the image of God carries with it great responsibility. When the apostle Paul attempted to establish the existence of God in the Book of Romans, he began with the creation.

For since the creation of the world God's invisible qualities — his eternal power and divine nature —have been clearly seen, being understood from what has been made (Romans 1:20, NIV).

God's character and attributes are made known throughout His creation. Creation in the Romans passage is the Greek word *ktisis* (ktis-is). Its meaning implies original formation of a thing, product, or creature. Implicit in the definition of creation is also the notion of proprietorship of a manufacturer.

The psalmist David wrote:

The heavens declare the glory of God; the skies proclaim the work of his hands. Day after day they pour forth speech; night after night they display knowledge. There is no speech or language where their voice is not heard. Their voice goes out into all the earth, their words to the ends of the world (Psalm 19:1-4, NIV).

Today much of our apologetic discourse begins with the Bible, but both David and Paul began with the creation. God identifies

Himself by what He manufactured. Before the Father embarked on the business of salvation, He was in the business of manufacturing and creating.

Your Creative Adventure

Another aspect of God's character or image is how committed He is to creating. Think about this for a moment. If God hadn't been committed to creating and manufacturing, we would not have known Him. God needed an adventure to actualize Himself. He needed to make something.

Dr. Paul Tournier defines adventure as "first a form of self-manifestation" and then describes five characteristics of adventure:

1. Adventure is a manifestation of oneself, a form of self-expression.

2. It innovates and invents; it is ingenious.

3. It is coherent, evolving in the pursuit of a single goal.

4. The goal is love; love suggests the goal, and love directs and sustains the adventure.

5. Finally, it involves risk.

Dr. Tournier has some valuable insights on creativity. Let's examine two of his quotes on this topic:

God manifests himself in his works, expresses himself in them, reveals himself in them. They are not independent of him like things one produces and then abandons when they are completed. They remain in him, and he in them, they are in his hand and continue showing forth His presence.... This function of self-expression has also been given by God to every creature, in an ascending scale corresponding to the scale of differentiation in creation.

Professor Arthur Jores, of Hamburg, spoke to us about what he called the diseases of man, that is to say, those which are peculiar to man, whereas many others are common to both human beings and animals.

The former, he said, are always connected with failure in self-fulfillment. The animal, impelled by instinct, cannot fail to fulfill itself. But in the case of man, the price of his liberty is that he can spoil his life and fail to fulfill himself. The frequent result is that he falls ill, not only physically, but also organically. The converse is also true, that self-fulfillment always has great therapeutic value.

This should not astound those of us who are familiar with biblical teaching. Proverbs 13:12 confirms these truths. Let's examine this verse from several different versions of the Bible:

Hope deferred maketh the heart sick: but when the desire cometh, it is a tree of life (KJV).

Hope deferred makes the heart sick, but a longing fulfilled is a tree of life (NIV).

Hope deferred makes the heart sick, but when the desire is fulfilled, it is a tree of life (Amplified).

No matter who you are and what your life experiences have been to this point, God has placed desire and ambition within you. God loves you too much to give you the prospect of hope only to embarrass you. Romans 5:5 says, "And hope maketh not ashamed; because the love of God is shed abroad in our hearts by the Holy Ghost which is given unto us." Ashamed in the Greek means to disgrace, dishonor, or confound. That is not God's will for you.

Dream the Impossible

Do you have a great big, seemingly impossible dream in your heart? God probably put it there. It will bring out His image in you. Don't be ashamed at this very moment to pursue it. Your hope is being ignited, you are coming alive so dance and sing. Call your friends and tell them that you are aroused from your slumber. Welcome that smile to your face; go ahead and giggle at that flutter in your heart; embrace this moment of epiphany.

Defer means to postpone or delay. To postpone the realization of the hope God has placed in your heart will make you sick with depression, despair, resignation, and defeat. When you are in this dangerous and carnal state, you are no good to God, others, or yourself. Hebrews 11:6 tells us that "without faith it is impossible to please him . . ." But what is faith?

Let's look at Hebrews 11:1 in some different translations:

Now faith is the substance of things hoped for, the evidence of things not seen (KJV).

Now faith is the assurance (the confirmation, the title-deed) of the things [we] hope for, being the proof of things [we] do not see and the conviction of their reality — faith perceiving as real fact what is not revealed to the senses (Amplified).

Now faith is being sure of what we hope for and certain of what we do not see (NIV).

If there is no hope in your heart, then there is nothing for faith to give substance to, and without faith you cannot please God. Romans 12:3 says, "God hath dealt to every man the measure of faith." The measure implies all you need. This faith will ignite the hope, the challenging, awe-inspiring dream that God has placed in your heart.

The ancient Greeks cherished exaggerated ideas of their own importance, but you need to have a sane estimation of the capabilities that God has given to you. Having a sane estimate of your abilities is relative and depends largely upon other variables. If you are a musician, artist, painter, surgeon, or zoologist, how much time do you regularly devote to the mastery of the skills needed in your profession? You can do great things for God — things that have a positive impact upon the world and bless many — without cherishing exaggerated ideas of your own importance.

Life is too big and the challenges too ever-present for me to think I can do it all alone. Since we are co-laborers with God, He needs us all functioning at optimal levels of faith and productivity. How do we do that?

Guard Your Heart

We think with our self-image, and that makes the activity of our minds very important. Proverbs 4:23 says, "Keep thy heart with all diligence; for out of it are the issues of life."

Keep is the Hebrew word *natsar* (naw-tsar), which means to protect or maintain; to watch, observe, and preserve with subtlety. Diligence is from the Hebrew word *mishmar* (mish-mawr), which literally means to post a prison guard, ward, or watch at the gate of your mind.

Why is this necessary? Because out of your mind flow the "issues," or sources, boundaries, outgoings, deliverances, and exits of life. The mind, which is the source of freedom, establishes the boundaries of our accomplishments for God. This is why we must diligently guard our minds at all cost. The mind thinks; thoughts become attitudes; and attitudes become belief systems that control our destinies.

Lowell Peacock David said, "Attitude is the first quality that marks the successful man. If he has a positive attitude and is a positive thinker, who likes challenges and difficult situations, then he has half his success achieved. On the other hand, if he is a negative thinker who is narrow-minded and refuses to accept new ideas and has a defeatist attitude, he hasn't got a chance."

McNally, in his wonderful book, *Even Eagles Need A Push*, writes, "Success begins the moment we understand that life is about growing; it is about acquiring the knowledge and skills we need to live more fully and effectively. Life is meant to be a never-ending education. When this is fully appreciated, we are no longer survivors but adventurers. Life becomes a journey of discovery, an exploration into our potential. Any joy and exuberance we experience in living are the fruits of our willingness to risk, our openness to change, and our ability to create what we want for our lives."

The heart (mind) affects the quality of our lives. One author writes, "We need to remember that most of our beliefs are generalizations about our past, based on our interpretations of painful and pleasurable experiences. The challenge is three-fold:

1. Most of us do not consciously decide what we are going to believe.

2. Often our beliefs are based on misinterpretation of past experiences.

3. Once we adopt a belief, we forget it's merely an interpretation.

We begin to treat our beliefs as if they're reality, as if they are gospel. In fact, we rarely, if ever, question our long held beliefs.... all of our actions are the result of our beliefs."

Renovation Underway

If we are going to get our lives unstuck, we must take responsibility for our belief systems. Romans 12:2 exhorts us to be "transformed by the renewing of your mind . . ." Our English word metamorphosis comes from the Greek word for transformed. The Greek word for renewing actually means to renovate. There will be no change in the quality of our lives until we begin to think differently, or until we renovate our minds.

In June 1991, the house my family and I were renting burned. We had to start a part of our lives over. The blaze injured our two year old son, and we lost most of our possessions. We had no renter's insurance and no savings. But God is faithful.

Our son fully recovered with very minimal scarring. All our needs were met. The fire destroyed the house, but the landlord had insurance. The insurance money enabled the owner to take that charred, water soaked house — with a giant hole burned through the roof — and renovate it. Because of the renovation, there is no trace that the house ever burned, except in our memories. Now that same house can provide shelter, warmth, and joy to another family, thanks to the power of renovation.

We need to understand that renovation is a lengthy process requiring a specific plan and the diligence and commitment of laborers to carry out the plan. In the case of that house fire, all the charred remains had to be removed before the renewing commenced. The same is true of our lives. God sends His Holy Spirit to remove the charred remains of the previous design. Then He offers a new plan for our lives. The Father has given Him carte blanche to carry out the work of renovation.

God the Father has signed a contract guaranteeing our restoration. I will cite two provisions here:

And I am convinced and sure of this very thing, that He Who began a good work in you will continue until the day of Jesus Christ — right up to the time of His return — developing [that good work] and perfecting and bringing it to full completion in you (Phil. 1:6, Amplified).

[Not in your own strength] for it is God Who is all the while effectually at work in you — energizing and creating in you the power and desire — both to will and to work for His good pleasure and satisfaction and delight (Phil. 2:13, Amplified).

Because of these promises, we can be confident that God is changing us from glory to glory and conforming us to the image of Jesus Christ. The renovation will last a lifetime, but we have the assurance that "when he appears, we shall be like him, for we shall see him as he is" (1 John 3:3, NIV).

Four Steps to Achieve Your Dream

William A. Ward has identified four steps to achievement:

1. Plan purposefully.

2. Prepare prayerfully.

3. Proceed positively.

4. Pursue persistently.

Nehemiah certainly incorporated these four steps in his life. Discovering that Jerusalem lay in ruins, he was able, by knowing his God, to rise to the challenge of rebuilding the wall of the city.

And it came to pass, when I heard these words, that I sat down and wept, and mourned certain days, and fasted, and prayed before the God of heaven.... And I said unto the king, If it please the king, and if thy servant have found favour in thy sight, that thou wouldest send me unto Judah . . . that I may build it.... So we built the wall; and all the wall was joined together unto the half thereof: for the people had a mind to work (Nehemiah 1:4; 2:5; 4:6).

Nehemiah enjoyed a comfortable and secure position in government. He certainly had no reason to lament the sad state of affairs in Jerusalem. Nehemiah, however, exemplified a major attribute of champions — they always have a vision bigger than themselves.

After conferring with the king, Nehemiah took a sabbatical to rebuild his beloved Jerusalem. Unable to do the work alone, Nehemiah had to convince many others of the expediency of his task and organize the volunteers to work together. While he raised enough finances to rebuild the once glorious capital of a nation, Nehemiah had to keep this work force motivated. As if that wasn't enough of a challenge, he also had to keep himself focused as the Sanballats and Tobiahs of the world tried to poison the morale of the people by discouraging them during the rebuilding.

Hard work and perseverance mark a true champion. Ernest Newman wrote, "The great composer does not set to work because he is inspired but becomes inspired because he is working. Beethoven, Wagner, Bach, and Mozart settled down day after day to the job in hand with as much regularity as an accountant settles down each day in his figures. They didn't waste time waiting for inspiration."

Nehemiah accomplished his goal of rebuilding Jerusalem in only 52 days, but it took much prayer and commitment to realize his dream.

Chapter 5

Dust Off Your Dreams

Ramona Banuelos, a Mexican immigrant, went from earning a dollar per day in a laundry to fulfilling her dream of owning a tortilla shop. Along with her aunt, Ms. Banuelos became so successful at making tortillas that other shops were opened. Over many years and after much hard work, these tortilla shops became Ramona's Mexican Food Products — at one time the largest Mexican wholesale food concern in the nation with more than 300 employees.

The same spirit of excellence that caused Ms. Banuelos to fight grinding poverty and human dream killers followed her as she moved forward to achieve success in business. She founded the Pan-American National Bank in east Los Angeles to serve the Mexican-American community. Even her own people thought she had assumed too big a challenge. Excellence caused her to persist. By the mid-1980s the bank's resources had grown to over $22 million with almost 90 percent of its deposits coming from Mexican-Americans.

Excellence means that you and I decide to become agents of change. We invest in ourselves through study, discipline, and commitment. A new America must be birthed in our spirits. You can run a profitable business. You are every bit as smart as Reginald

Lewis, an African-American who, at age 44, acquired TLC Beatrice International Holdings, Inc. for $985 million. Mr. Lewis' personal wealth before his death was said to be around $100 million.

Consider Madame C. J. Walker, an African-American, the first woman to develop a net worth of $1 million in the U.S. How about Mr. A. G. Gaston who went from earning 30 cents an hour in the steel mills of Alabama to a net worth of $40 million? These African-American entrepreneurs used their powers of choice to elevate themselves right out of poverty and lack.

Mr. Anthony Johnson, one of the original twenty Africans brought to America aboard Dutch slave ships, secured his freedom and went on to acquire vast land holdings and a respectable fortune. Mr. John H. Johnson, of Johnson Publishing Company, overcame racism, extreme poverty, and lack of education to turn a $500 loan into a worth of over $200 million. These great pioneers built their wealth without benefit of integration or affirmative action.

Building Big Dreams

Maybe you don't want to dunk basketballs, hit home runs, score touchdowns or goals, or even win Wimbledon. Maybe you want to build a corporation, practice law, become a highly-skilled neurosurgeon, govern your state, become president of a university, write books that sell millions, or be a preacher. Someone has blazed a trail for you in almost every area. Even if there is no trail, you blaze one! Go boldly where God's big dream in your heart leads you! Allow no one to steal or smother your dream. Remember, your dream is your potential.

Racism tempts one to become a destroyer versus a co-creator. I like what theologian Dorothee Soelle says about creativity. In her book, *To Work And To Love*, she writes, "Creative power is something we all have but often ignore or relinquish. My creative power is my power to renew the world for someone or for a community.

Through it, I attempt to rebuild the house of life out of the ruins in which we now live."

Remember, creative juices are boiling in you just beneath the surface. The image of God in you compels you to create. Don't say, "I can't..." You have enormous power as an individual. Exercise your power of choice. William A. Ward once said, "Adversity causes some men to break; others to break records."

History is filled with the seldom told stories of men and women of color who — in spite of racism, illiteracy, poverty, and sometimes precedent — have gone on to achieve greatness. This generation must not be robbed. No matter what the obstacles, we must strive for excellence. We must pursue the big dreams that God has placed in our hearts. We have a responsibility to leave fire on the hearths of our children's visions and dreams. We must leave them with more than anger, bitterness, and resentment.

I like what Dr. Dorothy Height, president of the National Council of Negro Women, asked over forty years ago: "What makes the great, great?" She then answered her own question, "Greatness is not measured by what a man or woman accomplishes, but by the opposition he or she has overcome to reach his goals."

I believe that the universe operates on the principle of law; the law of gravity, motion, etc. I also believe that human beings are subject to the laws that govern not only the physical universe but also those governing the realm of thought. Since our environment reflects our thoughts, if we control our thoughts, we control our circumstances.

This is why it is so important to carefully monitor all input to your mind. Everything that goes into your mind is either empowering or disempowering you. All input is either affirming or denying your greatness, either building or destroying your God-given big dream.

The Enemies of Greatness

In their valuable book, *Children of the Dream*, Audrey Edwards and Dr. Craig Polite write, "The invasive, collective sense of inferiority that often drives and thus debilitates the black race has been slavery's most enduring legacy." The dictionary defines inferiority complex as "a neurotic condition resulting from various feelings of inferiority, such as derive from real or imagined physical or social inadequacy and often manifested through overcompensation in excessive aggressiveness."

A sense of inferiority causes one or a group to react instead of being proactive. It is the enemy of greatness and long-term vision. To act based upon feelings of inferiority is to give an advantage to one's enemy. Only the redeeming love of God in Christ can bring a woman or man to a place of divine dignity and worth. Persons who experience a sense of inferiority cannot commit to excellence in any area, and they will not until a change in their thinking has been wrought at a deep level.

Mediocrity is the opposite of excellence, as John Gardner explains:

> As the individual contemplates the word "excellence" he reads into it his own aspirations, his own conceptions of high standards, his hopes for a better world. And it brings powerfully to his mind evidence of the betrayal of excellence (as he conceives it). He thinks not only of the greatness we might achieve but of the mediocrity we have fallen into.

Excellence is a commitment to a better world.

Matthew 5:9 says, "Blessed are the peacemakers, for they will be called sons of God" (NIV). The Greek word for peace is eirene. This peace is not merely the absence of war, but the presence of justice. *The Dictionary of New Testament Theology (Vol. II)* says, "Peace is the state of law and order which gives rise to the blessings of prosperity."

Do not think that this "law and order" refers to the laws of any nation per se. These are the laws of God that afford every person dignity and the right to prosper. The world suffers when a particular group of people takes it upon themselves to control the resources and wealth that belong to God.

The word *eirene* in *Strong's Concordance* means literally prosperity or to set at one again. Quietness and rest are also implied. Peacemakers are those who are committed to a "one again" world. Their commitment to prosperity reaches beyond the suburbs and corporate boardrooms of America to the ghettos, barrios, and reservations. Peacemakers do not want handouts. They do not believe in the inherent or supposed inferiority of any person or race. They understand the greatness of the peacemaker's vision.

Peacemakers understand that their vision is God's vision. Peacemakers, in their devotion to excellence, also understand the importance of team play. Personal growth is important to them, but also the growth and strengthening of all those around them. Peacemakers may be physicians, homemakers, CEOs, lawyers, teachers, athletes, managers, etc. No matter what their profession or vocation, they share a commitment to building a prosperous world for everyone.

Where the Air if Thin and Cold

My friend, Pastor Tony Morris of Seattle, has written a book on urban vision and leadership. His work refers to the Joshua Generation.

The Bible describes the succession of leadership from Moses to Joshua and then to Caleb as a powerful transition. All three were men of tremendous vision, faith, courage, and responsibility. These men believed in the possibility of the impossible. Each was part of a minority that did not believe in the inevitability of the present circumstances.

Excellence often beckons us to the Matterhorn of faith and possibility. The climb is steep and slippery, the air is thin and cold, the challenge is awesome and fearful, and you need expert help to climb. Tremendous odds say it cannot be done. Yet, the call for discipline is unrelenting, and excellence bids you come.

Mediocrity, on the other hand, requires little effort, as Norman Corwin suggests: "Mediocrity is, above all, comfortable. It makes modest demands on the powers of perception and ratiocination, and none at all on creativity."

Caleb walked in faith when the other spies doubted God's ability to bring them into Canaan. Even as an older man,

Caleb was quite visionary. I like what he said to Joshua regarding the division of the land.

> *"Now then, just as the Lord promised, he has kept me alive for forty-five years since the time he said this to Moses, while Israel moved about in the desert. So here I am today, eighty-five years old! I am still as strong today as the day Moses sent me out; I'm just as vigorous to go out to battle now as I was then. Now give me this hill country that the Lord promised me that day. You yourself heard then that the Anakites were there and their cities were large and fortified, but, the Lord helping me, I will drive them out just as he said."*

> *Then Joshua blessed Caleb son of Jephunneh and gave him Hebron as his inheritance. So Hebron has belonged to Caleb son of Jephunneh the Kenizzite ever since, because he followed the Lord, the God of Israel, wholeheartedly (Joshua 14:10-14, NIV).*

Vision kept Caleb alive into his eighties. He was driven by the promise of God. This kind of life-giving hope must be restored across America if our full potential as a nation is ever to be realized. Even though he had reached 85 years of age, Caleb was not thinking about dying; he asked for the mountain, the piece of land that had been promised to him 45 years earlier.

Where Excellence Begins

Excellence is not just for the business and corporate worlds. It is for neighborhoods and schools, churches, temples, synagogues, presidents, kings, prime ministers, children, senior citizens, and for people of all races from all over the globe. Profit for profit's sake is not the bottom line of excellence, neither is talent the primary prerequisite. Economic status and upbringing don't matter a great deal. Current educational levels, if viewed as inferior, are not irreversible liabilities.

We are all born with the seed of excellence inside us. You should be warned, however, that excellence stubbornly refuses to yield itself to petty ambition or cheap compromise. It answers the call of noble and lofty purpose. The Bible tells us, "If there is any virtue and excellence . . . think on and weigh and take account of these things — fix your minds on them." (Phil. 4:8, Amplified). Excellence begins in the mind.

Psychologists and theologians agree that our conversations and actions reflect our thoughts. Jesus Himself said, "out of the overflow of the heart the mouth speaks" (Matthew 12:34, NIV). Proverbs 8:6 says, "Hear; for I will speak of excellent things; and the opening of my lips shall be right things." Excellent in this verse is the Hebrew word *nagiyd,* meaning a high person, a leader, commander, noble one, a prince, an overseer, or king. In order to speak excellent things our hearts must be filled with them. There is nothing excellent about failure, defeat, despair, discouragement, lack, poverty, hopelessness, and resignation.

Another meaningful verse says, "Excellent speech becometh not a fool: much less do lying lips a prince" (Prov. 17:7). Excellence is from the Hebrew words *yathar and yether.* Both words connote jutting over or exceeding, abounding, to be plenteous, to excel and leave behind a remnant, to have superior excess or remains, to be plentiful. The proverbist tells us that these thoughts elude the fool. *Nabel* (naw-bale), the Hebrew word for fool, means wilted, failed, or fallen away. It also means disgraced, dishonored, lightly esteemed, or coming to naught.

The excellent spirit of the peacemaker understands that before a person can think excellent thoughts, he or she must be highly esteemed and honored. People who do not receive the honor and esteem that God wills for them become foolish in speech and deed. They become vile and come to naught or nothing.

We need a deep and abiding spirit of excellence in America, and true peacemakers must bring it about. This country or this world will never be all that God intends as long as we refuse to grant honor and esteem to each and every citizen, which is their divine birthright.

People who are withering and coming to naught do not contribute anything to the greatness of communities, neighborhoods, or nations. They do not see themselves as contributors, builders, leaders, decision makers, or change agents. The truth that all men are created in the image of God must be recaptured and heralded across the global village. Psalm 148:13 says, "Let them praise the name of the Lord: for his name alone is excellent; his glory is above the earth and heaven."

Hebrews 8:6 tells us that Jesus Himself was given a "more excellent ministry, by how much also he is the mediator of a better covenant, which was established upon better promises." Psalm 150:2 tells us to praise God "according to his excellent greatness." An excellent God always encourages His children to push beyond mediocrity.

The Demands of Excellence

Daniel was a man in whom was found a pre-eminent spirit, mind set, and attitude. "Forasmuch as an excellent spirit, and knowledge, and understanding, interpreting of dreams, and shewing of hard sentences, and dissolving of doubts, were found in the same Daniel.... Then this Daniel was preferred above the presidents and princes, because an excellent spirit was in him; and the king thought to set him over the whole realm" (Daniel 5:12; 6:3).

When the presidents and princes of the Persian government conspired to kill Daniel out of jealousy, his excellent spirit sustained him. Ultimately, Daniel's enemies became the victims of their own cruel connivance. What men intended for Daniel's destruction instead caused him to prosper because he remained true to his convictions.

Adversity is not always the end. Often it is the fertilizer for future greatness.

Excellence demands the following from you and me:

1. A clear and definite sense of purpose.

2. Acceptance of your own uniqueness and giftedness.

3. The hunger for continuous self-improvement in spirit, thoughts, emotions, etc.

4. Team spirit, or knowing there is no such thing as a self-made man or woman.

5. Acceptance of others by extending to them their dignity.

6. Freedom from fear of failure. Mistakes are part of life and some of its best teachers. When you fall, get up again and run to win.

7. Enjoy the true friendships that you have. True friends are rare. If God rewards you with many, it is cause to celebrate.

8. Accept change.

9. Honor God, yourself, and others.

In short, excellence is being all you can be. Dr. Charles Garfield has written, "Self-actualization is, in short, the tendency of every human being . . . to make real his or her full potential, to become everything that he or she can be. The self-actualizing person is the true human species-type . . . not a normal person with something added, but a normal person with nothing taken away."

The spirit of excellence summons forth all that is godly, great, noble, and determined in us. Dreams must be picked up and dusted off. Vision and hope must be restored. I know the road is long and haunted by many demons, but the quest for dignity, prosperity, and peace must compel us to complete the journey though weary and wounded. We must capture a new vision to transform ghettos, barrios, and reservations into places of human dignity, prosperity, and freedom.

Chapter 6

Becoming Fully You

One of the most painful periods in my life occurred when a member of the church where I serve as senior pastor betrayed me. Pastoral colleagues and personal friends cautioned me not to trust him. His past behavior supported the suspicions of my friends, but I forged ahead, all in the name of altruism. After all, I thought, everyone deserves a second chance.

Eventually, I permitted this brother to counsel married couples and teach a beginner's Christianity class. Because I wanted to foster cooperation between our workers and me, I chose to ignore my suspicions. Sometimes he and I disagreed, but that's not so abnormal.

My wife and I gave this individual all the encouragement and support we could. We invited him, his wife, and their large family to share our small three bedroom home with our three children. When he encountered even more financial difficulty, our small church, from which I did not even receive a regular salary, raised nearly $900 to assist him with delinquent bills.

To make a long story short, this individual showed up unannounced at my office the Monday following a moderate and albeit public confrontation the previous Sunday. Without even greeting me, he announced that I was teaching a false doctrine, and he and his family would no longer fellowship with us. This came during a turbulent and trying time in our ministry. Though not surprised by his action, I choked back the pain.

"How could he?" I asked myself. We had no previous discussion about false doctrine or any other disgruntlement, only repeated public and private pledges of faithfulness and loyalty. Now this.

This brother's actions caused a chain reaction in the church. People whom he had counseled took his side when I announced that he and his family would not be returning to our fellowship. After praying, crying, pouring over Scripture, and talking with my wife, I decided that it would not be good for those who desired to remain in our assembly to socialize with this family. We made an announcement to that effect, causing another chain reaction. Some of the people my wife and I nurtured through backslidden conditions, helped to get jobs, encouraged to attend college, and offered loans for tuition (which to date have not been repaid), decided to exit.

We had been committed to these people long before our now departed brother had ever come on the scene. They slept and ate in our home. We salvaged some of their marriages. Those whom we thought loved us and believed in our integrity before God now questioned us and abandoned us at a critical time. Talk about hurt!

We were angry, disappointed, and frustrated. I questioned God and the purity of my own motives. My stomach churned. I tossed on my bed at night, unable to sleep. We fought with all we had to be examples of faith and persistence. None of the those with whom we had stood so many times before offered any word of encouragement. In fact, we were accused of mismanaging church funds and carrying out personal vendettas against the brother.

My Healing Begins

It was difficult to pray, but I needed God's perspective. I wept before Him. Was I a failure? My wife and I felt emotionally raped and deeply wounded. During this time, an already successful church offered me a staff position. I assuaged my pain with thoughts of fresh ministry opportunities, but it was not to be. In addition to reading Scripture, I read another book that clarified my own values, rules, and an understanding of the source of my own pain. It also gave me practical, psychological reasons why I should forgive the ones who inflicted such injuries upon me and my family.

Tempted to be unforgiving toward these people, I knew my personal character hung in the balance. What would I do? The decision was mine. Would I stew for weeks, forcing my pain upon others, risking my health, and hurting the positive relationships I still had? Absolutely not! I chose to make an empowering decision.

I began to ask myself questions. What can I learn about myself from this? What might I have done differently? How can I go on in a positive direction, encouraging my wife and family? How can I strengthen those remaining members of the church who truly love us?

As I decided to be positive through this situation, I gained an immediate sense of empowerment. I felt in control of my destiny and of my emotional state. I decided not to be argumentative or defensive in discussing these matters with the offended ones. Most importantly, I decided not to become paralyzed by a host of toxic or negative emotions. I chose to be free!

Instead of looking at this situation as a disaster, I began to look for opportunities to grow and to strengthen my own character. Any situation is only as bad or as good as we perceive it. We decide whether we get good or bad out of any given experience.

F. W. Boreham said, "We make our decisions, and then our decisions turn around and make us." Kenneth Sollitt echoes that thought. "Freedom is the opportunity to make decisions. Character is the ability to make right decisions. It can be achieved only in a climate of freedom. For no one learns to make right decisions without being free to make wrong ones."

In order to build strong, godly character, we must consistently ask the right questions and make the right decisions. Brooke Foss Westcott offers this insight to character: "Great occasions do not make heroes or cowards; they simply unveil them to the eyes of men. Silently and imperceptibly, as we wake or sleep, we grow strong or we grow weak, and at last some crisis shows us what we have become."

Is Character Universal?

I think it's significant that the word character is not found in the Bible. Perhaps there is no such universal thing as character. Our actions stem from our thoughts, and our thoughts form our self-image. Character is very much a product of an individual's worldview. It emanates from how we see the world, God, ourselves, and others. Character is a self-esteem issue.

In the book, *Love, Medicine, and Miracles,* Bernie Siegel, M.D., writes:

Part of the mind's effect on health is direct and conscious. The extent to which we love ourselves determines whether we eat right, get enough sleep, smoke, wear seat belts, exercise, and so on. Each of these choices is a statement about how much we care about living. These decisions control about 90 percent of the factors that determine our state of health. The trouble is that most people's motivation to attend to these basics is deflected by attitudes hidden from everyday awareness.

Character, if it is an issue of self-esteem, is also an issue of choice. It is not a matter of imposing standards of response upon people that are incompatible with their values and belief systems. Decisions of character are made many times each day. Different responses to situations are expected and respected based upon environment and other factors. For example, in some communities it might be considered noble to verbally negotiate oneself out of a confrontation. In another community, this might be considered cowardly. Is one right and the other wrong?

Would universal character presuppose universal perception? Can there be a right thing to do that is right in every similar situation, regardless of the variables? We tend to act based on our own perception of a situation. One author suggests that every disagreement is a rule's disagreement. In other words, I am not offended by the act so much as I am offended because one of my basic tenets or rules for living has been violated. Your motive may not have been to violate my rules, but my rules may not have been compatible with your own. The place where we may look for character is not in the offense but in whether we choose to communicate why there was an offense in the first place.

Character could mean that you and I sit down and discuss the differences in our value and belief systems. From this we can learn how to more successfully communicate with one another in the future. When we think about character, traits like honesty, integrity, truthfulness, and respect come to mind. Virtue, valor, chivalry, and goodness may also constitute character to some people.

Character and Perception

Perception is critical to a discussion of character. Character is formed in the nuts and bolts emotional economy of everyday life. Character has a dialectic relationship with life and its challenges. Our perception of the world around us shapes our belief systems — and our beliefs may be the only reality for us.

In his elegantly evocative book, *Unconditional Life*, Dr. Deepak Chopra writes about perception:

Frustration and pain are trapped inside us by conditioning that tells us they are inescapable; therefore, to heal the pain, you have to go beyond the conditioning. We are all beset by limitations. The mind is structured around the impressions held inside it, and trying to deny or escape them is futile. Everyday a person thinks approximately 50,000 different thoughts, or so someone has calculated — a bewildering cascade of wildly mixed and conflicting impulses. In and of itself, this turmoil can be extremely painful. We feel true love and true hatred for the people closest to us, with seemingly no possibility of sorting one from another. The most destructive emotions — doubt, fear, guilt, shame, and loneliness — roam the mind at will, beyond our conscious control. It is truer to say that they control us. But this prison has an air of illusion about it once you realize that you built it and locked yourself inside. On one side, the old conditioning tells us that we will hurt worse if we try to break free. On the other, the impulse toward freedom is urging us to discover that all limitations are at bottom false.

Character may or may not be at the core of one's personal system of values. Authors and poets alike have written of man's eternal quest for meaning. When this most basic of needs is not met, one cannot expect a lot from his fellow man in terms of noble virtue and character.

Webster's Encyclopedic Dictionary defines character as "the aggregate of features and traits that form the apparent individual nature of some person or thing."

Churches all over America are filled each Sunday with nonselves — people who have dysfunctional and codependent relationships with religious doctrine, denominationalism, and church leadership. They lack spiritual depth and personal integrity and may possess only a partial view of salvation that aims at some religious notion of the forgiveness of sins but does not teach people to function in the real world. Such a view is shallow and dangerous.

Even some of the unchurched recognize and apply biblical principles. Human behavior experts, management specialists, and motivational speakers — many of whom make no profession of Christianity —make copious biblical quotes. And why not? After all, the Bible is the greatest book ever written on each of these subjects.

Broken Trust

The Greek philosopher Diogenes made himself most unwelcome in Athens by trudging about barefoot without wearing a proper robe. He carried a lantern around during the day, thrusting it into the faces of fellow Athenians, and declared, "I am looking for a man, an honest man." He is said never to have found the man.

In a previous chapter, we discussed self-esteem or self-image. Self-image, the mental picture we carry of ourselves, encompasses our values, rules, fears, habits of response and communication, goals and dreams — or lack of the same. Self-image is also the way we view the past, present, and future.

The decisions we make based on our self-image constitute our character. Particular mental and emotional states and our responses to them illuminate our character.

While the word character is not found in the Bible, Scripture has much to say about the dispositions of a man's heart. Character is not some nebulous entity. The Bible says character flows out of a man's heart. Macaulay once said, "The measure of a man's real character is what he would do, if he knew he would never be found out." Even secular institutions understand the value of character. Part of the U.S. Air Force Cadets' Honor Code oath says he will "not lie, cheat, or steal, nor . . . tolerate anyone who does."

Lack of character sabotages personal and professional relationships. It ruins businesses, churches, and careers. The absence of truth, honesty, and integrity has caused emotional and financial destruction and is responsible for the unforgiveness that grips untold numbers of people around the world.

Many of you have experienced pain inflicted by someone's lack of integrity: a loved one who jilted you, a dishonest business partner, a fellow Christian in whom you trusted. I encourage you not to be too hard on them. The ones who hurt you may never have given any thought to personal values and rules for living.

Maybe you grew up in a family that valued trust. You gave and received it freely. Now you are in a relationship with a person from a home where there was no trust, only suspicion and condemnation. The potential conflict becomes obvious. Trust is an important value or rule for you and your relationships but not for the person with whom you are involved.

You've Got All You Need

Now that we've discussed character and its relationship to self esteem, let's look at God's provision for us in this beautiful passage of Scripture:

Grace and peace be yours in abundance through the knowledge of God and of Jesus our Lord. His divine power has given us everything we need for life and godliness through our knowledge of him who called us by his own glory and goodness. Through these he has given us his very great and precious promises, so that through them you may participate in the divine nature and escape the corruption in the world caused by evil desires.

For this very reason, make every effort to add to your faith goodness; and to goodness, knowledge; and to knowledge, self-control; and to self-control, perseverance; and to perseverance, godliness; and to godliness, brotherly kindness; and to brotherly kindness, love.

For if you possess these qualities in increasing measure, they will keep you from being ineffective and unproductive in your knowledge of our Lord Jesus Christ.

But if anyone does not have them, he is near-sighted and blind, and has forgotten that he has been cleansed from his past sins. Therefore, my brothers, be all the more eager to make your calling and election sure. For if you do these things, you will never fall, and you will receive a rich welcome into the eternal kingdom of our Lord and Savior Jesus Christ (2 Peter 1:2-11, NIV).

Everything we need to transform ourselves into that marvelous, awe-inspiring creature God destined us to be is already inside us. God's divine power and promises are the keys to unlocking the prison doors to our real self and finding contentment and the peace of knowing that the eternal kingdom is already ours to inherit. What glorious truth! This is the key to happiness and fulfillment.

The apostle Peter gives us eight building blocks of character: faith, goodness, knowledge, self-control, perseverance, godliness, brotherly kindness, and love. For those who believe in the relevance of biblical numerology, the number eight represents resurrection and regeneration — the birth of a new order. In Hebrew the number eight is *sh'moneh* from the root *shah'meyn*, "to make fat, cover with fat, to super-abound." The participle form means one who abounds in strength. The noun form means super-abundant fertility, or oil. Both fat and oil in Scripture represent prosperity, favor, wealth, health, and great blessing in general.

God hides such potent nuggets of revelation in His Word. The Father has not only promised to make our lives fertile, but He tells us how to do it. Praise God for a fertile life. You can always plant in fertile soil and expect a crop.

Finding Your Ecstacy

No book on personal success or human improvement and potential surpasses the Bible. There, we read of lives transformed in an astounding and miraculous fashion.

You are already a miracle, the handiwork of God. He took the time to mold and shape you in His image and He wants you to succeed in life. God wants you to find your ecstasy. One of my favorite words, ecstasy means alive and full of passion, color, sound, and motion.

I looked up the word passion in the dictionary and found, to my surprise, that most of the definitions were negative. This one, however, almost captures the essence: "a strong or extravagant fondness, enthusiasm, or desire for anything . . ." God is both passionate and extravagant. Inasmuch as God often exceeds the bounds of reason in His actions, opinions, and passions, He may be called extravagant. During the six days of creation, I don't believe God yawned. He was absolutely thrilled, intoxicated with joy and laughter, festive and celebratory. Leon Bloy has said, "Joy is the most infallible sign of the presence of God."

What has happened to the church? We must get words like wow, outrageous, splendid, magnificent, passion, extravagant, beautiful, luxurious, incredible, wonderful, and tremendous back into our vocabulary!

You are made in the image of God. Go ahead, find your passion. Thirst for the exquisite. Accept the wonder of you. Commit to the eight building blocks of character. Nurture your fertility, which encompasses everything — your mind and body, dreams and desires. Allow yourself the gifts of passion, extravagance, and joy.

A Joy for Living

When I think of character, passion, and joy, a dear friend of our family comes to mind. Doris, then in her late sixties, died a few years ago from a rare form of cancer. In our city of under 50,000 people, hers was an unofficial state funeral. Almost 700 people attended, including our mayor, police chief, members of our city council, county commissioners, and several other prominent civic, business, and professional leaders. I was humbled and deeply honored when Doris' husband Blaine, a very prominent man in the community, asked me to conduct both her graveside and memorial services.

Doris was one of God's most special people. Even after her last surgery, which was extremely debilitating, she continued to make everyone around her feel special. Doris was an unabashed party person who often called our home, looking for an excuse to throw a party. She loved people, food, joy, and laughter, and most importantly she had a deep commitment to the Lord.

Our friend Doris was one of the few people I have ever met who genuinely did not see color when she looked at people. She never said, "I don't see color when I meet people." You just knew that she was genuine. She didn't want any dirges played at her memorial services. Colorful flowers, balloons, bagpipes, and praise choruses marked her passing from this life into glory.

Because of the strength of her Christian commitment, her joy for living, and all the lives she touched, Doris left behind a legacy of godly women and men of different ages to carry on her work. These people are from different theologies and traditions, but they are all people of prayer who deeply love the Lord and are committed to His work.

With her body in great pain from the last surgery, which removed part of her clavicle, Doris attended a banquet held in honor of my wife Shelley and me. With Blaine by her side, Doris strode to the podium, and with courage, dignity, and unrelenting wit, proceeded to wrench tears from everyone present. We knew this was a special moment.

Maybe Doris was an angel. It wouldn't be hard for me to believe.

From the deck of their lovely home overlooking the breathtaking splendor of Puget Sound, Doris was visited by a very special friend. Her love of eagles was no secret, and shortly before her homegoing she received the gift of eagle splendor. A large bald eagle swept into her view, spiraling, ascending, sealing her joy. We thank that eagle for obeying God, and we thank Doris for all she means to us. We have concluded that she is now in charge of all parties being planned in heaven, so you don't want to miss them. They will be a treat!

If You're Hurting

I know Doris' cheerful spirit and continuous generosity warred against the cancer in her body for years and allowed her to continue ministering to others while she herself endured great pain. She lived the truth of Proverbs 17:22: "A cheerful heart is good medicine, but a crushed spirit dries up the bones" (NIV).

What of those who do not know such joy, who have not come to appreciate the wondrous gift of serving? What of those who know not such nobility of character, whose lives are daily tormented with despair, depression, loneliness, fear, and rejection? Remember the eight building blocks of character found in the Bible.

God loves you so much that He has already given you all you need to live a life filled with value, dignity, character, fulfillment, passion, and joy. Find God's plan for you and know that joy is very legitimate in the kingdom of God. Discover and study God's laws for successful living — like the laws of thought, supply, attraction, receiving, increase, compensation, non-resistance, forgiveness, sacrifice, obedience, and the law of success itself.

In their lovely book, *Passion for Life*, Muriel and John James write:

Like the urge of plants toward sun and water, there is always an irresistible urge within us for growth. Whether the plants live in lush grasslands of open fields, in dry and barren deserts, or on wild and windy mountain peaks, they always strive to grow. In a way we are like plants as we too are challenged to grow, regardless of who we are or where we live.

These irresistible stirrings to do something are due to universal urges that come from the depths of the spiritual self. They reveal the functions of the human spirit and seek to be released in the form of meaningful goals.

The James tell us that we are born with seven basic urges: to live, to be free, to understand, to enjoy, to create, to connect, and to transcend. Perhaps that ache in your soul is there to let you know that you are still alive. That's your passion waiting to be given focus.

Maybe what you feel is a kind of anxiety. Psychotherapist and author Rollo May has defined anxiety as "the experience of being affirming itself against non-being." Dr. May assures us that "anxiety is essential to the human condition."

Respond to the Genius Within

Most of us think character has to do with how we treat others — whether or not we are kind, loving, truthful, patient, and so on. What about the courage to confront our own genius, our own God-given spark and passion? That requires tremendous character.

In *Courage to Create*, Rollo May writes, "If you do not express your own original ideas, if you do not listen to your own being, you will have betrayed yourself. Also you will have betrayed our community in failing to make your contribution to the whole." The world needs your ecstasy, your passion, your genius. Decide now to rechannel the energy you've used to deny your genius into discovering and cultivating it!

Robert Grudin, author of *The Grace of Great Things*, writes, "Original thought is the product not of the brain, but of the full self. And self, as I understand it, is not confined by our skins but defined by our humanity." He comments further that "if anything controls or dominates at the moment of inspiration, it is not the mind but the idea, or rather, the suddenly articulated power of our own inner energies. New ideas capture and possess the mind that births them; they colonize it and renew its laws. The expansion of any idea is thus an expansion of the self." Finally, Professor Grudin tells us that "because it is a radical act of freedom, creative achievement is a heroic process that requires . . . specific strengths of character."

Do you realize that character is not only how you treat others but how you respond to your own God-given genius, gifts, and talents? Take a risk and push yourself beyond those self-imposed limitations. President Theodore Roosevelt said, "Far better it is to dare mighty things, to win glorious triumphs, even though checkered by failure, than to rank with those poor spirits who neither enjoy much nor suffer much, because they live in the gray twilight that knows not victory or defeat."

Go ahead and dream big — it's a key to a more fulfilling life. The Pennsylvania School Journal printed this thought-provoking quote: "The poorest man is not he who is without a cent, but he who is without a dream." It's true.

Remember, God wants you to be a partaker of His divine nature. He desires that we grow in our knowledge of Him. "The people that do know their God shall be strong, and do exploits" (Daniel 11:32).

You are made in God's image. Because He is identified by His creation, so are we, as 2 Corinthians 3:13-15 makes clear:

Every man's work shall be made manifest: for the day shall declare it, because it shall be revealed by fire; and the fire shall try every man's work of what sort it is. If any man's work abide which he hath built thereupon, he shall receive a reward. If any man's work shall be burned, he shall suffer loss: but he himself shall be saved; yet so as by fire.

God created then judged His creation, and so shall He judge yours and mine. Passion compelled God to create, and it longs to do the same with us.

Goleman, Kaufman, and Ray in their volume, *The Creative Spirit*, companion to the PBS television series, state, "Creativity begins with an affinity for something. It's like falling in love." God set in motion a universal law — the law of use. You must use your potential. Until you do, you are not fully you. God continually uses His potential, thus He is always actualized. He is never less than God. This is why God said, "I the Lord do not change" (Mal. 3:6, NIV).

We, however, are changed into the image of Christ who was totally surrendered to His divine purpose day by day. Each day we are creating! At the end of each creation period, are we able to look back at our creation and call it good? If not, we can change through the power of the God who loves us and knew us from before our birth.

Chapter 7

Pray Big!

Prayer is infinitely more than a hollow religious exercise. It deeply involves the realms of imagination and creativity. Some have described prayer as a conversation with God. This is true, but it is also incomplete. I believe that God intends prayer to reestablish a harmony between man and wisdom, and through wisdom, between man and himself. Ultimately, God desires harmony between man and the creation. Proverbs says this about wisdom:

The Lord by wisdom hath founded the earth; by understanding he hath established the heavens. By his knowledge the depths are broken up, and the clouds drop down the dew (Prov. 3:19,20).

Get wisdom, get understanding: forget it not; neither decline from the words of my mouth. Forsake her not, and she shall preserve thee: love her, and she shall keep thee. Wisdom is the principal thing; therefore get wisdom: and with all thy getting get understanding. Exalt her, and she shall promote thee: she shall bring thee to honour, when thou dost embrace her (Prov. 4:5-8).

Jesus encourages us, "Ask, and it shall be given you; seek, and ye shall find; knock, and it shall be opened unto you" (Matthew 7:7). Among other things, Scripture tells us to ask for wisdom. "If any of you lacks wisdom, he should ask God, who gives generously to all without finding fault, and it will be given to him" (James 1:5, NIV). Most of us have a grossly anemic understanding of wisdom. The wisdom of God's Word is far too powerful to be trifled with and wasted upon dead religiosity.

The Hebrew language will help us to see some of the many facets of wisdom. One word for wisdom is *chokmah* (khok-maw), meaning to be and act exceedingly wise in mind, word, or act; to be skillful and witty. The word *tuwshiyah* (too-shee-yaw) is rich. It means to substantiate or support; ability in purpose; intellectual understanding; or an enterprise, which in itself is substance and sound wisdom working. The word *biynah* (bee-naw) deals with discernment and means to consider, be cunning, informed, instructed; to look well into, to be a skillful teacher-thinker so as to cause others to get understanding. The word *leb* (labe) speaks of the heart, the feelings, the intellect or the mind. Finally, the word *sekel* (say-kel) means circumspect and intelligent. It also means to be an expert in knowledge and policy, and to have good success.

God used this wisdom to fashion and sustain our universe with its innumerable intricacies. This wisdom, which is creative and imaginative, plumbs the depths of the mind of God. It is also inexhaustible and available to the common man. This wisdom does not come from any university but begins with the fear of the Lord.

Knowing God involves so much more than what organized religion has traditionally offered. God offers wisdom in prayer. The Father of all creation wants to do more through prayer than merely make us feel good. He longs to reveal His plans and purposes to us.

The Kingdom Within

Prayer is power for living. The disciples saw Jesus heal the sick, feed multitudes, and raise the dead. Jesus transformed lives everywhere He went. Seeing this power in action, one of the disciples said, "Lord, teach us to pray, just as John taught his disciples" (Luke 11:1, NIV). Jesus responded:

When you pray, say: "Father, hallowed be your name, your kingdom come. Give us each day our daily bread. Forgive us our sins, for we also forgive everyone who sins against us. And lead us not into temptation" (Luke 11:2-4, NIV).

This prayer, known as the Lord's Prayer, offers a framework for our relationship to the Father in worship and devotion. It also deals with the coming of the kingdom of God, which Jesus says "is within you" (Luke 17:21).

What did Jesus mean when He said that the kingdom of God is within you? We know that God's kingdom is His realm, His place of rule and dominion. Psalm 24:1 says, "The earth is the Lord's, and everything in it, the world, and all who live in it" (NIV). The entire universe — visible and invisible — is the realm of God's rule. He created it and owns it all. Before God created this universe, was there anything for Him to rule over? Before God created the universe, it was "within Him." In other words, the universe was His potential.

The apostle Paul wrote that God's power and nature are known through His creation.

The wrath of God is being revealed from heaven against all the godlessness and wickedness of men who suppress the truth by their wickedness, since what may be known about God is plain to them, because God has made it plain to them. For since the creation of the world God's invisible qualities — his eternal power and divine nature — have been clearly seen, being understood from what has been made . . . (Romans 1:18-20, NIV).

God has a purpose for everything that He created, including you and me.

For we are God's [own] handiwork (His workmanship), recreated in Christ Jesus, [born anew] that we may do those good works which God predestined (planned beforehand) for us, (taking paths which He prepared ahead of time) that we should walk in them — living the good life which He pre-arranged and made ready for us to live (Ephesians 2:10, Amplified).

Nicodemus, a wealthy and prominent man, visited Jesus at night to inquire about the miraculous power being manifested all about Palestine. Jesus replied, "I tell you the truth, no one can see the kingdom of God unless he is born again" (John 3:3, NIV). The word "see" means to discern, distinguish, or understand. The source of Jesus' power was the kingdom of God, which resided within Him. Jesus Himself said, "The words I say to you are not just my own. Rather, it is the Father, living in me, who is doing his work" (John 14:10, NIV).

Know Who You Are

Scripture tells us, "Yet to all who received him, to those who believed in his name, he gave the right to become children of God — children born not of natural descent, nor of human decision or of a husband's will, but born of God" (John 1:12,13, NIV). We do not have to pray as strangers if we have believed in His name.

Jesus was an extension of the Father's plan. He came to earth not to marvel in the natural beauty of Palestine but to reclaim His Father's creation. Jesus' early understanding of sonship and purpose greatly impacted His prayer life. Jesus knew that He had come to destroy the works of the enemy — the poverty, the pain and suffering, the injustice and inhumanity, all the evil in the world. He keenly understood the kingdom of God and the availability of its power to accomplish the Father's desires. Jesus gave us insight into the relationship between the kingdom of God, sonship, purpose, and power.

Jesus also said:

Believe me when I say that I am in the Father and the Father is in me; or at least believe on the evidence of the miracles themselves. I tell you the truth, anyone who has faith in me will do what I have been doing. He will do even greater things than these, because I am going to the Father. And I will do whatever you ask in my name, so that the Son may bring glory to the Father. You may ask me for anything in my name, and I will do it (John 14:11-14, NIV).

Jesus understood that the Father was at work in Him. The Father planted the kingdom of God inside the bosom of Jesus, and the Son's prayer life largely consisted of looking into that kingdom, discerning the Father's will, then doing what He saw the Father doing.

What We Call "Miracles"

Almost all discussions on prayer are by nature subjective. It could be argued that prayer must subscribe to the laws of the universe and that answers to prayer will always fit within that framework. The term "laws of the universe" is not intended to be synonymous with natural law. We must allow for those laws not yet known, or for what we call miracles.

The apostle Paul tells us that we "know in part" (1 Cor. 13:12). Perhaps when we know in full, we will discover that what we thought were miracles only seemed so to our incomplete knowledge of the laws of the universe.

The apostle Paul wants us to know God — and His power — in a life-changing way. He penned one of my favorite passages of Scripture:

I keep asking that the God of our Lord Jesus Christ, the glorious Father, may give you the Spirit of wisdom and revelation, so that you may know him better. I pray also that the eyes of your heart may be enlightened in order that you may know the hope to which he has called you, the riches of his glorious inheritance in the saints, and his incomparably great power for us who believe. That power is like the working of his mighty strength, which he exerted in Christ when he raised him from the dead and seated him at his right hand in the heavenly realms, far above all rule and authority, power and dominion, and every title that can be given, not only in the present age but also in the one to come (Ephesians 1:17-21, NIV).

This is power for living. It is the power that raised a dead man to resurrected, immortal life. It is the very power of life itself. How unselfish and loving of God to make this power available to all who believe in His name. Know it, imbibe it, drink deeply from this fountain.

God's power toward you is incomparably great. Prayer seeks this power and the specific purpose for which it is to be used. God's power and His kingdom are in you and me. We must know His purposes in order not to live barren and unfruitful lives. It is not the will of God that we spend our days in boredom and mediocrity.

Called to Greater Works

Do you know what the Father is doing in you? Many give a standard answer such as, "He's causing me to grow." We know that, but grow into what? What does the Father want you to create, to birth? Do you know how God wants you to potentialize? Until you release your potential, you are only potentially you. What invisible things in your life are waiting to be made visible to prove that you are a child of God?

We have relied too much on personal testimony to convince others of who we are. We need to be able to say with Jesus, "Believe me for the very works' sake" (John 14:11). Jesus performed incredible deeds and gave the credit to the Father. We can do the same — and we must!

Jesus also said this about prayer: "Have faith in God,. . . I tell you the truth, if anyone says to this mountain, 'Go, throw yourself into the sea,' and does not doubt in his heart but believes that what he says will happen, it will be done for him. Therefore I tell you, whatever you ask for in prayer, believe that you have received it, and it will be yours" (Mark 11:22-24, NIV).

This passage is awesome. Jesus tells us that if we ask for something and believe we have already received it, it will be ours. Upon hearing this verse taught, many people immediately begin to nullify it by saying things like, "Well, you know we're just a bunch of old miserable sinners and our desires are wicked. We'd surely ask God for the wrong things." So we think we are being spiritual by asking God for nothing and sparing ourselves rebuke and chastisement.

Cultivate Your Desire

The Holy Spirit is sounding a wake-up call. He longs to respond to your prayers in amazing ways, but we must throw off religion, which has a form of godliness but denies its power. What does God say about the desires He has planted in your heart?

The desire of the righteous ends only in good (Prov. 11:23, NIV).

What the righteous desire will be granted (Prov. 10:24, NIV).

The desire accomplished is sweet to the soul (Prov. 13:19).

He fulfills the desires of those who fear him; he hears their cry and saves them (Psalm 145:19, NIV).

Maybe the desire in your heart is so big that you just can't believe it's possible to attain. This is wonderful. You need God's help — the activation of His divine power. What is wisdom calling forth from you?

Remember, before God created the universe, it resided in His mind or heart. Proverbs 8 tells us that wisdom called forth and co-created the universe. Many believe that God's work of creating is done. I do not share this belief. If God were through creating, we would have no desire in our hearts. Desire is often bred by purpose. It not only glorifies God when accomplished but also brings spiritual, emotional, and physical health.

Medical science tells us that having a reason to live is a powerful healing force in the treatment of various diseases, including cancer. Desire bred by purpose and nourished by discipline will extend your life and improve its quality. Unfulfilled desire leads to depression, which affects the brain and body.

Studies show that the neurotransmitter catecholamine is depleted during depression. This results in increased secretion of endorphines (the body's own morphine), which signals the immune system to shut down. When this occurs, the human body is much more susceptible to disease of all kinds, including cancer. Not pursuing the desire God has placed in your heart may shorten your life and drastically affect the quality of those years you do have.

Pray Big Prayers

Pray big and ask according to the desire in your heart. See it through the eye of your imagination in vivid color. Smell it, taste it, touch it, hear it, but above all, see it. John Ruskin wrote, "The greatest thing a human soul ever does in this world is to see something.... To see clearly is poetry, prophecy, and religion, all in one."

In prayer you may only ask for what you can vividly imagine. Diane Ackerman in her tasteful book, *A Natural History of the Senses*, writes, "Our language is steeped in visual imagery." This is why in prayer you may only ask for what you have developed the ability to see.

How richly are you willing to allow the Holy Spirit to fertilize your imagination? The Holy Spirit brooded over the darkness, chaos, and confusion of pre-creation. God responded to this need. He was so pregnant with the universe that all He had to do was say, "Let there be light," and there was light. God richly imagined light, vegetation, flora, fauna, mountains, oceans, and the solar system with such intensity that when He spoke their names, they burst forth.

The power of creativity and imagination working with the law of faith replaces darkness and chaos with light and order. God saw it and believed it, so it had to be. He is the same God today. When we get His desires in our heart and see what He is doing, we will pray big and then say it is the Father in me who does the work.

Jesus operated by this principle. He prayed to know the Father's mind and intent. Then through His faith He released the power to accomplish those works. The prayer that Jesus instructed His disciples to pray in Luke 11 also dealt with social relationships and personal character. Though this prayer is brief, it is comprehensive.

We often get hung up on the form of prayer instead of its power and content. Those just developing the discipline of prayer often ask if they should pray sitting or standing, kneeling, with folded hands or open palms, or with eyes open or closed. Men and women of God in the Bible used many different postures. I know of no verses that mandate folding the hands or closing the eyes. Some biblical characters prayed in the temple; some prayed outside. Some prayers were short; some quite long.

When people become legalistic about prayer, discouragement soon sets in and their attempts at prayer are short-lived. Posture is not nearly as important as actually praying and allowing the Holy Spirit to direct you.

God's Purpose or Your Plans?

We have focused on the dimensions of prayer that speak of faith, imagining, the kingdom of God, creativity, and so on. We now come to another very important aspect of prayer. Proverbs 19:21 says, "Many are the plans in a man's heart, but it is the Lord's purpose that prevails" (NIV). You must be committed to God's purpose for your life, even above your own plans.

Praying with purpose often leads to direct confrontation with the powers of darkness. Remember Jesus in the wilderness? (See Luke 4.) In order to fulfill His mission, Jesus had to confront Satan himself. The devil tried Jesus' motives and tempted Him with diversions, which represented illegitimate power and false blessing, in other counterfeit purposes.

Jesus knew He had to endure the cross to fulfill His purpose. In the Garden of Gethsemane, Jesus' humanity expressed great anguish of soul coupled with a desire to avoid the agony of the cross. Ultimately, however, Jesus submitted His will to the Father. Jesus the man, the Word made flesh, yielded His will in spite of the same temptation to disobey and take the low road that plagues you and me.

We often excuse our weakness, saying, "After all, Jesus was the Son of God." This is dangerous and hypocritical. We often use Jesus' divinity to justify our temptation. In His frail humanity Jesus resisted temptation and submitted His will to the Father although it ultimately cost Him His life.

One of the most comforting verses in the Bible for me is Hebrew 5:8: "Although he was a son, he learned obedience from what he suffered" (NIV). Jesus learned obedience through His personal suffering.

Many people have been suffering all their lives and still have not learned to submit their lives to a caring and loving God. People suffer from poor self-image, anxiety, codependence, sexual frustration, bitterness, boredom, depression, and unfulfillment.

Often the internal conflict becomes so intense that a person feels that suicide is the only answer. The victim has learned to see herself or himself as helpless and surrenders the will to live.

I believe that at the moment Jesus surrendered His will to the Father, He was filled with an enormous power. Making the right choice propelled Him toward the completion of His mission.

We all need a powerful, compelling reason to live. We need impossibilities to conquer. They will demand that we surrender. The realization of God's will for us demands that we experience our own Gethsemane and learn obedience. You and I must confront the demons that want to destroy us through counterfeit purpose, resignation in life, or suicide.

Many have committed suicide because they were convinced of the impossibility of the desire God had placed in their hearts.

Nothing Is Impossible!

I believe that giftedness in all people, whether they know God or not, yearns to be released. God says with Him all things are possible.

Nothing is impossible with Him. Did you get that? It is impossible to be linked with the God of the universe and pull off nothing! The only thing that is impossible with God is nothing!

Someone once said, "Power concedes nothing without a demand." Jesus' mission was to be the Savior of the world. The Gethsemane prayer released Him into the fulfillment of that mission.

Jesus could have decided not to obey the Father's purpose for Him. Can you imagine Jesus running through Palestine telling everyone, "I was supposed to be the Savior of the world, but I blew it in the Garden of Gethsemane. I made the wrong decision." If that had happened, where would you, I, and all the world be?

Don't surrender to suicide, depression, illegal drugs, perverted sex, neurosis, or withdrawal. Pray big! Ask God, "Who am I, and why?" Then when He tells you say, "Not my will, but thine be done." Then arise empowered to accomplish the will of God. Redeem the gifts and talents, the power and energy God has given you. Allow your creativity and imagination to be released by the Holy Spirit.

Anguish of the magnitude that Jesus experienced in the Garden caused Him to potentialize as the Savior of the world. The most agonizing period in the life of Christ catapulted Him into the fulfillment of His purpose.

Perhaps you are experiencing the most difficult and distressing period of your life. That could very well be God telling you to break out of the box. Maybe you have kicked and screamed, rejecting the desire God has placed in your heart. You protest, "It's too big. I don't have the faith. I could never accomplish this." But another part of you screams, "I can't take another day of this boredom! I want to create something. I have a big, God-glorifying dream and I long to give birth to it. I want to sing and dance, to give someone some joy, to bless someone. I want to do something better for my family."

Something in your repressed self wants to shout, "Hallelujah!" You want to buy streamers, party favors, balloons, and food and for no apparent reason call all your friends and throw a fantastic party. The old you quickly objects, "That's the weirdest thing I have ever heard! My friends will think I'm crazy, and they probably wouldn't come anyhow."

You're not crazy, and I guarantee that your friends will come to the party. People love parties. Secretly they've wanted to do something spontaneous but haven't had the courage. Go ahead, don't be afraid of joy. Luke 12:32 says, "Do not be seized with alarm and struck with fear, little flock, for it is your Father's good pleasure to give you the kingdom!" (Amplified).

Prayer has delivered people from seemingly insurmountable situations. God's love for you is no different than it was for all those who called upon Him for deliverance in Bible times. Scripture says, "The prayer of a righteous man is powerful and effective. Elijah was a man just like us. He prayed earnestly that it would not rain, and it did not rain on the land for three and a half years. Again he prayed, and the heavens gave rain, and the earth produced its crops" (James 5:16-18, NIV).

James used the great prophet Elijah as an example that God hears the prayers of ordinary men. But, you say, Elijah was anything but ordinary. You're right. He was not afraid to pray very big prayers. Elijah knew God, and he prayed according to God's ability not his own inability.

Have you and I been praying according to God's ability or according to our own perceived inability?

Dreams Not Fantasies

Throughout the Bible, vision and prayer have transformed common, everyday men and women into city, nation, and world changers.

Vision, faith, prayer, and hard work transformed a group of former slaves into the nation of Israel. On their way to nationhood, they crossed the Red Sea and desert (complete with serpents and scorpions). They had to overcome disenchanted people who harbored contempt for the responsibility of nation building. Great prayers and great vision imply great responsibility.

Proverbs 21:25 says, "The sluggard's craving [desire] will be the death of him, because his hands refuse to work" (NIV). A lazy woman or man will never pray great big prayers because of the responsibility.

He who works his land will have abundant food, but he who chases fantasies lacks judgment (Prov. 12:11, NIV).

He who works his land will have abundant food, but the one who chases fantasies will have his fill of poverty (Prov. 28:19, NIV).

There is no need for a child of God to chase after fantasies. The language of the Holy Spirit is dreams and visions, not fantasies. (See Joel 2:28.) Dare to believe God for the kind of vision that will grip you and direct your life — and be prepared to take responsibility for that vision.

God gave Adam responsibility for the Garden of Eden, that lush and incomparably beautiful paradise that provided for his every need. Adam violated the rules of oversight of the Garden, thus forfeiting his purpose and setting God's plan of redemption in motion.

Whenever God births something through you, He gives you responsibility for it. You must oversee it and assume dominion over it.

Adam was entrusted with the earth and blew it. Jesus was entrusted with redeeming earth and mankind. Because He obeyed, assumed responsibility, and continues to pray, men and women are still coming to know God. Ultimately, the creation will experience redemption.

Doing the Impossible

Even though Jesus had cultivated a lifestyle of prayer for years, He faced a time when things looked awfully grim. The secular and religious authorities sought His life. Many of His most ardent followers abandoned Him. Judas, one of the men Jesus had personally trained, sold Him for 30 pieces of silver. Arrested for crimes He did not commit, Jesus was tried and sentenced to death. His most trusted friends forsook Him, letting Jesus go to the cross broken, mocked, and rejected.

Jesus' character shone in these debilitating circumstances. In the midst of incredible pain, Jesus prayed, not for Himself, but for His executioners. One bystander taunted Jesus with vinegar to quench His torrid thirst. A Roman soldier thrust a spear into Jesus' side. Having asked God why He was forsaken at so critical a time, He convulsed and drew His last breath.

Are you at a place in your life where you feel forsaken by loved ones? Maybe you are experiencing the trauma of divorce. Maybe you recently lost a loved one and feel as though you cannot go on. Perhaps you feel so depressed that you contemplate overdosing on pills or putting a gun to your head and ending it all. You may have been told all your life that you are a nobody destined for nothing. You feel defeated every day of your life. You have no joy in living. Maybe you chase fantasies and don't believe that you are capable of anything great. You find yourself unskilled and can't muster the courage and energy to do anything about it.

If any of these descriptions fit you, I have good news. Find a private place. It might be your bedroom, your favorite park, or a spot on the beach. You may be curled up in front of a crackling fire. Wherever you are, I want you to stop and pray right now. Pray big and strong. Pray with faith. Allow God to love you, to affirm you, and to give you a vision. See a new future filled with bright and bold possibilities.

Remember the words of Jesus: "With man this is impossible, but with God all things are possible" (Matthew 19:26, NIV).

Chapter 8

When You Blow It

I know how embarrassing failure can be. Once I auditioned for the lead role in a community theater production of "Purlie," the once-famous play by African-American actor/playwright Ossie Davis. The thrill of being chosen quickly faded during weeks of grueling rehearsals.

On opening night friends and acquaintances, who had come to see the first African-American drama in our community theater's history, filled the audience. Backstage the cast, which by now had grown very close, battled opening night jitters. Much to our relief, opening night went off without a hitch, and the positive reviews elated us.

In a subsequent performance, during one of the most crucial scenes, I completely forgot my lines. When a sudden case of amnesia strikes, what does one do? Realizing I had drawn a blank, my co-star began to laugh; then the audience caught on and began to laugh. This continued for about three minutes; then we briefly ad-libbed and continued. That performance ranked as one of our best.

That evening taught me a valuable lesson. I knew the way I handled this embarrassing situation would affect our cast and the audience. Laughter proved to be our salvation. Completely unrehearsed, laughter — not tears — was the right thing. Choosing to laugh, when we could cry, frees us from paralyzing anxiety.

Often we personalize failure and devaluate ourselves based upon one episode. I wonder how many would have beens stand on the sidelines somewhere because they were never taught to handle failure.

H. Ross Perot has said, "Most people give up just when they're about to achieve success. They quit on the one yard line. They give up at the last minute of the game, one foot from a winning touchdown." Is this the story of your life? Perhaps you fumbled the ball on fourth and goal with seconds left in the game and your team down by three points. The other team recovered and your team lost. Or maybe you came in fifth place at the science fair after working so long and hard on your project.

No person persists at anything when he sees himself as a failure. Having grown up as a perfectionist, I know my mistakes are the stuff that makes horror movies. My tape of negative self-talk automatically played whenever I made a mistake. "You're so stupid — a real klutz!" this inner voice berated. As a result, I often started projects but never finished them.

After making a mistake and taking personal responsibility for that phase of the failure, projects become the enemy. I find it difficult to separate myself from my methods. Maybe I need a mentor, or better information. Perhaps I don't have quite the proper work environment or don't understand thoroughly the task at hand. These may explain the reason for my present failure. Why must I, or anyone else, punish myself in this situation with negative self-talk? Negative self-talk only erodes confidence and instills fear.

Have specific incidents from your own life come to mind? Perhaps times when you put yourself down, or others put you down, for something that could have been a learning experience. Failure is not permanent, but not everyone knows this. People live in mental institutions or walk the streets of America as manic-depressives because their inability to handle failure pushed them over the edge.

Motivated by Fear or Faith?

Psychologists tell us that our response to circumstances has more to do with our perceptions than the facts intrinsic to the event itself. What we think about an event, person, or thing shapes our reaction. This being true, failure may be considered to be "in the mind."

Many people do not achieve happiness or true fulfillment in life because of fear. Fear of failure; fear of success; fear of sickness; fear of dying, but also fear of living. The Bible says, "fear hath torment" (1 John 4:18). The salvation offered to the human race by God through His Son Jesus Christ grants liberation from the gnawing, destructive power of fear.

God did not create man to live his life in fear and failure. It simply is not God's will. We will never do exploits for God and humanity if we live under stifling fear. The key to overcoming fear and other poisonous emotions is by the "renewing of your mind" (Romans 12:2). We must undergo a massive thought revolution.

In both of Dr. Benjamin Carson's books, *Gifted Hands and Think Big,* he credits his mother with his success. When he was doing anything but achieving success, his mother continued to plant good, positive seeds in his mind. Today, though he is still a young man, Dr. Carson is a fine role model for people of all ages and a legend in the field of neurosurgery.

John Johnson in his book, *Succeeding Against the Odds,* says, "There's an advantage in every disadvantage, and a gift in every problem." More often than not we're taught to focus on the problem or the disadvantage. Mr. Johnson, an African-American man, who didn't have the benefit of a college or high school education, overcame racism, grinding poverty, and a host of human dream killers. He built the Johnson empire, consisting of *Ebony* and *Jet* magazines, with a $500 loan from his mother. Mr. Johnson's empire also includes Fashion Fair beauty products and stores.

Fear will prevent you from *carpe diem,* seizing or getting the most out of the day. Ecclesiastes 9:10 says, "Whatever your hand finds to do, do it with all your might, for in the grave, where you are going, there is neither working nor planning nor knowledge nor wisdom" (NIV).

I do not believe that the force of faith is released until one gets a dream, a vision — some great big hope. Perseverance, persistence, and patience are needed. But none of these matter if there is no faith. Faith actually is not invisible; it is the substance of the invisible. Once faith is released to manifest the invisible, it requires patience to complete its work.

Don't Give Up!

The gravitational energy of the whole earth is estimated to amount to only a millionth of a horsepower. A toy magnet in the hands of a child can be thousands of times stronger. But what gravity lacks in brawn, it makes up in tenacity. Its reach is limitless; it shapes and governs the universe across unimaginable chasms of space. Its frail attraction keeps the moon orbiting the earth, the planets revolving around the sun, and the sun — along with a billion other stars — rotating around the center of our galaxy like a cosmic pinwheel.

To produce one pound of delicious honey, the honey bee must fly the equivalent of three trips around the world. Worker bees who cannot find a nearby nectar source fly as far as eight miles to find one. The worker bee sees neither time nor distance. He has the goal of finding nectar and returns to the nest only after the mission has been accomplished. Thomas Edison once said, "Work is not measured by hours, but by what it accomplished."

Persevere until you reach your goal. One story says Johannes Brahms took seven years to complete his famous lullaby because he kept falling asleep at the piano. Josh Billings has said, "Consider the postage stamp: Its usefulness consists in the ability to stick to one thing till it gets there."

James 1:4 says, "Perseverance must finish its work so that you may be mature and complete, not lacking anything" (NIV). Whatever you do, find your purpose and pursue it passionately. Don't quit! Understand that failure is the grace of God to teach you the right and wrong ways to do things. After every failure I'm smarter and better equipped.

Don Owens, Jr. said, "Many people fail in life because they believe in the adage: If you don't succeed, try something else. But success eludes those who follow such advice. Virtually everyone has had dreams at one time or another, especially in their youth. The dreams that have come true did so because people stuck to their ambitions. They refused to be discouraged. They never let disappointment get the upper hand. Challenges only spurred them on to greater effort."

The Bible repeatedly talks about diligence. Proverbs alone has much to say about this subject:

Lazy hands make a man poor, but diligent hands bring wealth (Prov. 10:4, NIV).

Diligent hands will rule, but laziness ends in slave labor (Prov. 12:24, NIV).

The sluggard craves and gets nothing, but the desires of the diligent are fully satisfied (Prov. 13:4, NIV).

The plans of the diligent lead to profit as surely as haste leads to poverty (Prov. 21:5, NIV).

All hard work brings a profit, but mere talk leads only to poverty (Prov. 14:23, NIV).

The discipline of staying with your goals will bring great things to pass in your life. The biggest obstacles will fall in the face of perseverance. Remember, it's always too soon to quit.

Obey Your Destiny

Don't be afraid to take some risks and go for it! All my life I've wanted to be a writer. One day it occurred to me that as long as I merely wanted to be a writer, I would never become one. Having chosen to pursue my goal, I have determined not to be satisfied with average. I read a variety of authors, noting their style and rhythm. I peruse not just books, but newspaper and magazine articles. I am going to get better and better on purpose.

Thank God for the many writers who have come before me — writers of verse and prose; of fiction, history, and biography. Many of them have shared their early struggles and frustrations. Author Robert Benchly said, "It took me fifteen years to discover that I had no talent for writing, but I couldn't give it up because by then I was too famous."

If you are alive, you have not accomplished your mission on earth. Abraham Maslow said, "A musician must make music, an artist must paint, a poet must write, if he is to be ultimately at peace with himself." The key word in this quote from Maslow is *must*. We give ourselves too many choices at the wrong time. You must accomplish your desire; it is God's will that you do.

Maslow's quote, obviously, is not exhaustive. Apply it to the dream in your heart. Know that your peace will come only as you obey your destiny. I believe chaos to be any state other than divine intent. Anything existing in a state outside its purpose is in chaos.

Within you and me is not only the purpose intended for us, but the ability to discover the purpose for other things and to create things to which we give purpose. You must absolutely know the following things:

1. You are valuable and valued. (Scientists tell us that because of the potential energy charge of our bodies, each of us is worth around $85 billion.)

2. You have a divine purpose and destiny.

3. God has given you all the faith you need to accomplish this purpose.

4. Divine resources are available to you.

5. It is God's will that you prosper.

6. You are not a failure!

Finally, understand that perseverance requires discipline. Everything in the universe functions in accordance with some set of laws. To succeed, the laws of your purpose demand absolute submission before they will reward you. He who comes to God must believe that He rewards those who "diligently seek him" (Hebrews 11:6).

Your hiatus is over. No more sabbatical. It has been said, "Excuses are the tools with which persons with no purpose in view build for themselves great monuments of nothing." Decide today that you will make no more excuses for where you are in life — or where you want to go. Perseverance will get you there.

Chapter 9

Created to Be Healthy

Twenty percent, a full one fifth of Americans, are obese. Many of them can be found sitting in the churches of America. These wonderful people love God, their fellow man, and church functions surrounding food. Who hasn't felt a twinge of guilt for overindulging in barbecued spare ribs, potato salad, and peach cobbler at the last church picnic? Overeating, however, is just as much a problem in the pulpit as it is in the pews.

How many preachers leave their churches on Sunday for the hospitality of some member for "fellowship"? The same preacher who railed against lying, infidelity, and gossip may sit down to a platter of golden fried chicken, collard greens soaked in pig fat, several slices of cornbread oozing with butter, macaroni and cheese, Kool-Aid or iced tea loaded with sugar, and, for dessert, another sugary concoction made with bleached flour and more fat. After a feast rivaling those of King Henry VIII, God's great mouthpiece looks for the nearest place to lie down and digest his blessing.

I am not trying to be self-righteous. I love fried chicken and Haagen Daaz ice cream, but enjoying these high-fat, high cholesterol foods gradually added 40 pounds to my frame. I understand the discomfort of carrying extra weight. My clothes seemed to shrink, and I had to look for bigger sizes.

At age 35, I started a regular exercise program, lost the weight, and now feel great. My waist, which had ballooned to 39 inches, is back down to 32. My suit size, which was 48, is back down to 40. Believe me, it is extremely gratifying. I no longer eat a pint of Haagen Daaz at one sitting. I eat one helping of my favorite foods and have eliminated the burgers, fries, and Pepsi.

If anything, I want this chapter to encourage you. If I can do it, so can you.

Why Eat Right?

Dr. John McDougall writes, "People are meant by nature to be healthy and active. However, it is obvious that most of us who live in modern and developed societies fall short of that ideal. We are tired, and overweight, and we take a multitude of pills for various ailments. The calculated life span of a person is approximately eighty-five years, and each decade of life should be filled with activity and the continuing ability to see, hear, taste, move, and think. In reality, people living in western nations degenerate as they progress toward premature death. If our natural condition is supposed to be good health, then why is illness so prevalent in our society?"

All the controversy over the so-called "health and wealth" gospel in recent years is short-sighted. Most of these arguments fail to take into account the relationship between diet and health. Health is the will of God. Whether you call it divine health or not is unimportant. Health is the will of God, and healing exists to restore health. Scripture says, "May God himself, the God of peace, sanctify you through and through. May your whole spirit, soul and body be kept blameless at the coming of our Lord Jesus Christ" (1 Thess. 5:23, NIV).

In 1939, Jethro Kloss published a book entitled Back to Eden. In this book Mr. Kloss wrote:

Overeating or too frequent eating produces a feverish state in the system and overtaxes the digestive organs. The blood becomes impure, and the diseases of various kinds occur.... Overweight people are much more likely to have a serious illness than those who maintain a normal weight. Cancer of the breast and womb, kidney disease, diabetes, gallstones, osteoarthritis, arteriosclerosis, high blood pressure, and apoplexy (strokes) are some of the consequences of overeating. Obese persons frequently have high levels of cholesterol and triglycerides in their blood and are much more likely to die suddenly of a heart attack.

In his book, *The McDougall Plan,* Dr. John McDougall writes, "There is no subject of greater physiological importance, or of greater moment for the welfare of the human race, than the subject of nutrition." The apostle Paul wrote, "in view of [all] the mercies of God, to make a decisive dedication of your bodies — presenting all your members and faculties — as a living sacrifice, holy (devoted, consecrated) and well pleasing to God, which is your reasonable (rational, intelligent) service and spiritual worship" (Romans 12:1, Amplified).

I know that we worship "in spirit and in truth" (John 4:24, NIV), but presenting our bodies as holy and well pleasing sacrifices is also an intelligent form of worship. Why do we treat our bodies any way we want and think we can dodge the consequences? We eat the wrong foods, neglect exercise, don't get adequate sleep, and still believe we are spiritual.

Eat Well, Feel Well

Medical research also supports the fact that emotional states such as depression, stress, and apathy may be caused by improper diet. Brian and Roberta Morgan write in their book, *Brain Food,* "Neurotransmitters have a profound effect on the way you feel, and the specific behavior patterns you exhibit in everyday life. They also affect your physical health: directly, through physical changes, and indirectly through mood changes. People who have little control over their moods appear to suffer more from diseases of all types. So, controlling your emotional nature has a physical side effect."

Since I have eliminated certain foods from my diet, I am far less stressed and impatient and experience far greater peace.

You may think, Yes, but the foods that are good for me don't taste very good. Broccoli, asparagus, spinach, ugh! This is only as true as you think it to be. Vegetables, when prepared properly, are delicious, nutritional, and filling. You don't have to become a vegetarian. Instead of fried meats, try some baked or broiled chicken or fish. Avoid fried foods as much as possible. It's okay to enjoy a piece of fried chicken every now and then, but make sure that you don't fry in animal fat.

Studies also show a clear link between diet and criminal activity. In the introduction to Alexander Schauss' book, *Diet, Crime, and Delinquency*, Michael Lesser, M.D. writes:

Ordinary foods, or the lack of them, can alter our mind, much like alcohol or unleashing criminal behavior. How does this happen? Our brain is no different than the rest of our body. Brain cells require proper feeding to function correctly. In fact, the brain is the body's most chemically sensitive organ. Starved for the right nutrients, or "gummed up" by toxic pollutants, the brain can and does go haywire.... sugar starvation, vitamin deficiencies, lead pollution and food allergies can convert a normal brain into a criminal mind. Dostoevsky used the term, "brain fever"; in fact, food allergy can "inflame" the mind, creating the conditions for a crime.

Dr. Lesser adds, "Working with heroin addicts in Harlem in 1968, he (Schauss) noticed that those able to kick their diet of fast foods, colas and refined sugar improved, while those who stuck in a 'junk food' rut continued to use narcotics. At that time, I was in charge of a narcotic rehabilitation program. We found that physical exercise relaxed the addicts and reduced their craving for narcotics. We also observed that when the men and women were withdrawn from heroin, they developed voracious appetites. The combination of wholesome food, adequate in protein, with daily intense physical exercise turned pale skinny junkies into ruddy faced, healthy, happy men and women."

Harmful Substances

Poor diet, lack of exercise, and inadequate sleep may also harm the inutero development of children, along with the proven harmful effects of tobacco, nicotine, and alcohol.

Nicotine reaches the brain only eight seconds after the smoker has inhaled. Other tissues and organs absorb nicotine, decreasing its level, so the smoker craves another cigarette to raise the brain nicotine level. Nicotine in the brain also increases dopamine and norepinephrine levels, along with electrical activity levels, making the smoker alert and less irritable.

Smoking also stimulates the hypothalamus, reduces the appetite, and relaxes the muscles. Nicotine is in the same family as heroin, mescaline, morphine, strychnine, and quinine. If you smoke one pack of cigarettes a day for a year, you will have received 50,000 doses of a drug in the same family with heroin.

If you're addicted to nicotine, I understand your frustration. I smoked cigarettes for over a decade, ending a two-pack-per-day habit in 1980. I quit cold turkey — and so can you. You may need some additional help, and that's fine. Whatever you do, in the name of health and life, please quit.

Caffeine, a stimulant, is found in everything — from your favorite chocolate delights to coffee, some teas, and cola drinks. Doctors tell us that consuming more than 350 mg of caffeine per day causes physical dependence. I can testify to that! Not long ago I had to have a twelve-ounce coffee every morning — with no less than four packets of refined white sugar. Now I enjoy sooth-ing herbal teas sweetened with honey.

Caffeine consumed in doses of 600 mg or more daily leads to depression, anxiety attacks, insomnia, stomach upset, etc. Too much caffeine also overstimulates the brain and may lead to iron deficiency. Excessive caffeine consumption may also cause im-paired fetal growth.

Like caffeine, alcohol's effect upon the brain and body depends upon the quantity consumed. The effects of alcohol range from euphoria with small amounts to loss of memory and death with larger doses. Drinkers may experience impaired vision, loss of coordination, impaired driving ability, coma, as well as loss of memory, concentration, and insight. Increased alcohol consump-tion may also lead to violent mood swings and uncontrollable outbursts of anger.

If you or someone you know has four or more drinks of hard liquor daily, they are destroying virtually every part of their mag-nificent brain. Alcohol also leads to serious vitamin and mineral deficiencies. Fear of fetal alcohol syndrome should deter all preg-nant women from drinking. Breast-feeding moms should know that alcohol gets into the milk. The myth of alcohol assisting milk flow must be debunked. The truth is that alcohol inhibits milk flow.

For those who must consume tobacco, caffeine, and alcohol, you may want to consider minimizing your risks with vitamin therapy and diet, but the wisest policy is to abstain from harmful sub-stances.

Preventing Disease

We often give more consideration to the clothes we wear than the foods, medicines, and other substances we ingest. Believe me, what we eat is far more important. Each of us needs to decide whether or not to eat packaged, preprocessed foods or chemically laden meat and dairy products.

One myth says it's much more expensive to eat healthily. In our home, the monthly food bill has been drastically cut by eliminating non-nutritious processed foods. Many Americans believe meat to be the only, or at least the best, source of protein. Vegetables, such as legumes, are actually a much better source of protein than meat.

Diseases such as diabetes, hypoglycemia (lowered blood sugar), ulcers, arthritis, kidney stones, gall stones, hypertension (high blood pressure), anemia, asthma, and salmonellosis may be prevented by making wise dietary choices. Salmonellosis has been called one of the most important communicable disease problems in America today. Every year over four million cases of this disease occur. Salmonellosis, a bacterial infection derived from contaminated animal products, results in nausea, diarrhea, stomach cramps, fever, vomiting, and chills. This disease can be fatal among the elderly and infants with their weakened or underdeveloped immune systems.

Several very important books on the market, such as John Robbins' *Diet For A New America*, expose the myths concerning the nutritional value of milk, eggs, and dairy products. Look for Frances Moore Lappe's *Diet For A Small Planet* and the writings of Dr. John McDougall.

God's Perspective on Food

God said to Adam, "I give you every seed-bearing plant on the face of the whole earth and every tree that has fruit with seed in it. They will be yours for food" (Genesis 1:29, NIV). God also gave laws regarding clean and unclean foods. (See Leviticus 11.)

The king of Babylon singled out Daniel and Hananiah, Mishael, and Azariah for conscription into the Babylonian way of life. Their captors immediately tried to alter the diet of these Hebrews. "The king assigned them a daily amount of food and wine from the king's table. They were to be trained for three years, and after that they were to enter the king's service" (Daniel 1:5, NIV). But listen to Daniel's appeal for a dietary change:

> *But Daniel resolved not to defile himself with the royal food and wine, and he asked the chief official for permission not to defile himself this way. Now God had caused the official to show favor and sympathy to Daniel, but the official told Daniel, "I am afraid of my lord the king, who has assigned your food and drink. Why should he see you looking worse than the other young men your age? The king would then have my head because of you."*

> *Daniel then said to the guard whom the chief official had appointed over Daniel, Hananiah, Mishael and Azariah, "Please test your servants for ten days: Give us nothing but vegetables to eat and water to drink. Then compare our appearance with that of the young men who eat the royal food, and treat your servants in accord with what you see."*

> *So he agreed to this and tested them for ten days. At the end of the ten days they looked healthier and better nourished than any of the young men who ate the royal food. So the guard took away their choice food and the wine they were to drink and gave them vegetables instead (Daniel 1:8-16, NIV).*

Diet is important to God. I am not attempting to build a theology of food. Unhealthy eating and lack of exercise will not keep you out of the kingdom of heaven. It will, however, radically alter your quality of life while you are on this earth.

Little Profit in Exercise?

The scripture most often used to justify an undisciplined physical lifestyle can be attributed to the apostle Paul. He wrote, "For bodily exercise profiteth little: but godliness is profitable unto all things, having the promise of the life that now is, and of that which is to come" (1 Timothy 4:8).

According to historians, the man who made this statement was quite a sports fan. Many of the figures of speech used in Paul's letters come from the world of the Greek Coliseum and the Olympiad games of Greece. The Greek athlete, a highly trained and disciplined individual, competed in grueling sports. Greek athletic contests differed from American sports in that the rules applied only to the training. There were no rules once Greek wrestling or boxing contests began.

Paul's statement to Timothy must be taken in context. Relative to eternity, bodily exercise pales in significance and provides little profit, but Paul did not mean, "Neglect your bodies. We're all going to heaven anyway."

The contemporary culture of Paul's day did not encourage sedentary lifestyles. The masses worked outside in the Mediterranean sunshine and performed physically stimulating labor. Except for the wealthy classes, diet was not centered on meat. Inordinate fat, cholesterol, and "junk food" did not exist. Absent were the stresses of living in our 20th century technopolis. The world of Paul and Timothy differed greatly from our own.

Let me add a disclaimer. No one is being scolded or recruited into diet and exercise fanaticism, but small overtures in both directions increased over time will bring noticeable, beneficial results.

See Yourself Healthy

Eighty-five million Americans are overweight, which is directly attributed to eating too many of the wrong foods and not getting moderate amounts of regular exercise. When was the last time you had a complete physical examination? Have you intended to join that health club only to procrastinate? Have you discussed the need to change your eating and shopping habits with your family?

We procrastinate when we really haven't decided to change our behavior. Feeling overwhelmed by an enormous task, we procrastinate.

Maybe you have quite a bit of weight to lose, and the prospect of how long it's going to take — and the anticipated pain of exercising — is just too much to bear. I've got good news for you! The pain/pleasure principle can motivate you in the right direction. Almost all our actions are taken either to avoid pain or to gain pleasure. If you can associate more pain with not losing the weight or changing your family's eating habits, and more pleasure with having a healthy family and a slimmer body, you will take action.

Sure, the kids yelp when they learn there will no longer be meat at every meal and that ice cream will come on rare occasions, if at all. Believe me, children can learn to love fresh fruit instead of sugary and fatty treats. They can learn to enjoy fruit juices instead of colas and Kool-Aid.

A church in your community may offer aerobic classes during the week at a minimal cost. Men, aerobics is not just for the ladies. It is ideal if husbands and wives can exercise together, but our schedules sometimes make that impossible. If you're having difficulty getting started, you should know that smart eating and regular exercise will also enhance your sex life.

Don't be afraid to set goals in these areas. Visualize yourself as thin and energetic. Imagine yourself eating healthy foods and enjoying them. Remember, "as he thinketh in his heart, so is he" (Prov. 23:7). It has been said that where the mind goes, everything else follows. Eat to nourish and fuel your body, not to satisfy hunger that is more mental than physical.

Getting Started

Exercise does not have to be painful hard work. Aerobic exercises are important inasmuch as they stimulate blood and, thus, oxygen flow. ATP (adenosine triphosphate) is the basic energy for whatever the body does. We breathe 2500 gallons of air daily to get the oxygen our cell tissues need. This oxygen assists the cells in burning glucose and producing ATP. Regular exercise has many other positive benefits.

Many experts have written extensively on diet and exercise. Get started by visiting a bookstore, preferably one located in a health food store, and buy a couple of books on proper diet. If the person working there is a healthy eater, ask her or him some questions. People enjoy sharing their expertise. You may even make a new friend.

Next, visit your physician. If your doctor isn't fit, he or she is not the one to ask about exercise. You don't have to change physicians if this person's skills and competence in other areas are proven. I believe in professional and personal loyalty, but when it comes to exercise, get a competent opinion. Next, establish some clear-cut goals, pray, draw a deep breath, and get started.

A final caution: If you are going to do aerobics, run, play tennis, basketball, or any other sport that is hard on the feet, make sure you have the proper footwear. Don't worry about being a fashion plate. Comfortable, functional footwear will do just fine. Now go get 'em, tiger!

Chapter 10

Wealth — God's Gift

God's original intent for man — prosperity — has not changed. More than enough wealth exists in the earth to provide prosperity for everyone on the planet. America's inner cities and Third World nations experience poverty, homelessness, declining access to adequate health care, cycles of despair, heightened crime rates, and drug and alcohol abuse. These conditions exist contrary to the will of God.

At the same time a minority amasses personal fortunes that only grow by day. I do not condemn personal wealth, only make a plea for the wise and humane use of it. Despite the disparity we see in the world, we should not become fatalistic concerning our economic situation. The Bible comforts us with these words: "But many that are first shall be last; and the last shall be first" (Matthew 19:30).

The topic of biblical prosperity puts the reputation of Almighty God on the line. We acknowledge God as universally loving without respect to geography or race. William W. Wells describes God's gracious intent:

The Bible begins with a wonderful picture: an exuberant God creating a bountiful world filled with fruitful vegetation, animals, and

waters teeming with fish. When his world was complete, God cre-
ated a man and a woman and placed them in the midst of this abun-
dant world. All creation was theirs. And he gave them this gift.
God commanded Adam and Eve to be fruitful themselves, to multi-
ply, and to take care for his creation.... God intended Adam and Eve
to enjoy his creation and that it would supply their needs com-
pletely.

Some wealthy people do all they can to ameliorate the suffering of the world, but they cannot do it alone. Corporations must get involved with the motive of improving the quality of life for all citizens of the earth.

My faith is strengthened when I reflect upon the God who de-livered Israel from the slavery of Egypt. God called a group of slaves, who had experienced the degradation and stifling of the human spirit, to conceive and build a humane government.

Dr. Myles Munroe says that when the purpose of a thing is not known, the abuse of that thing is inevitable. Certainly the world has gone askew in understanding the purpose of wealth. Those who horde wealth as protection against an uncertain future have not sufficiently learned the lessons of history.

Politicians say the budget will be balanced in 1997. This is doubt-ful unless God is brought into the economic picture. God, for all practical purposes, disappeared from the public life of Americans in the 17th and 18th centuries. Some seriously argue whether He was ever involved. I realize the Bible's advice on economics comes from the perspective of an agrarian and provincial system, but the fundamental humaneness and compassion of the system can be applied today.

Participating in the Future

Poverty is not an inevitable financial, psychological, and social reality. This is where the church must assume a major leadership role in the present and future. Economics, of necessity, must come within our view. Trends must be studied, which will allow leadership to give visionary direction to those who must cope in an increasingly sophisticated world.

The "when we all get to heaven" attitude is not going to cut it in the quickly changing, technologically challenging world of the 1990s. How are we going to equip people to participate in the future? By 1995, 43 percent of all jobs in this country will be related to the information industry.

In his provocative book, *God The Economist*, M. Douglas Meeks writes:

> *It is true that most human beings will feel that the relationships of power, property, work, and consumption in which they live are forced upon them, that they have no essential control over them. But the prevailing modes of these components of political economy have been produced by human values and decisions shaped by the rudimentary faith of masses of people. No particular political economy exists for long without fundamental support of its assumptions by most of the people among whom it flourishes.*

Meeks' statement is profound in that it tells us people are accomplices in their own economic woes to a large extent. Are the alarming statistics regarding various ethnic groups caused by chronic despair and malignant defeatism? Big problems have the potential to summon forth the greatness of a people or a nation. Like the sons of Issachar, "who understood the times and knew what Israel should do" (1 Chron. 12:32, NIV), we must be able to discern spiritual seasons and know what course of action to take. But we can't do it alone. The excellence of team commitment can really make a difference. Think tanks and/or consortiums must be begun along with resource banks.

During Arsenio Hall's former late night talk-show, several gang members announced on national television that a truce had been declared among their own group. Simultaneously they pledged to try and reach their unconverted homeboys so that the violence and mayhem might cease.

Contrary to popular opinion, these men and women are not illiterate thugs and losers with a bestial bent toward killing and destruction. Many of them possess phenomenal management and leadership skills; some are bright and articulate. I believe gang members have as much potential as anyone in this society, but they must acknowledge and dialogue with their anger. At the same time, society must respond to the causative environmental conditions that give rise to that anger. Poverty is undoubtedly one of those causative factors.

Jacob Needleman has written, ". . . to emphasize the illusions and corruption of man's existence without clearly envisioning his nearly godlike possibilities is to live in a nightmare."

Harsh Realities

Poverty is much more than the material condition of lacking money and/or resources. It is a spiritual and psychological reality that can and does lead to pathological antisocial behavior. The Hebrew language has several words for poverty. *Yaresh* (yaw-raysh) means to rob, consume, or destroy; to dispossess, disinherit, expel or utterly drive out without fail; to utterly seize upon. *Reysh* (raysh) means to soften or mollify; to be fainthearted or weak. *Chacer* (khaw-sare) implies failure, want, lessening; to be in a state of bereavement; to decrease, fail, or be made lower; a state of destitution. The Greek word *ptocheia* (pto-khi-ah) means beggary or indigence.

I believe that the psycho-spiritual dimension of poverty can and does induce madness — not anger, mind you, but madness. I define madness as an induced state of hyper-dysfunctionality, leading inevitably to destructive behaviors or to suicide. The dysfunctionality manifests itself in the form of rage. This rage is a sign that the victim is not only alive but has chosen to live. This rage will not be brought under control by platitudes, sloganizing, or demagoguery, whether political or spiritual.

As I observe the contemporary scene, it appears that a large measure of this rage is directed toward repossessing one's humanity. It is not, nor has it ever been, the intention of God that a minority of the world's population would control access to the world's resources. Nor did He desire that they simultaneously control the humanity and the fate of the remainder of the world's population. We need to carefully listen to the cry of the people that their heritages be respected and included with the traditions and history of the world. But it is more than that.

I believe that a free market economy strongly undergirded by an economics of compassion allows for the most profound expression of human potential. African-Americans, poor whites, or other ethnic groups, however, must never consent to the idea that wealth and privilege are the birthright of the elite.

Money is only one indicator, and not always a true one, of wealth. Our lives today are almost totally consumed by money. In his book, *Money and the Meaning of Life*, philosopher Jacob Needleman wrote, "Money is, at the present moment in history, the principal means by which we attain respect from others and is, therefore, the principal means of social self-respect."

This statement certainly should not shock anyone. Those who control wealth and resources potentially may manipulate the destinies of others. First, however, those non-wealth controllers must internalize the rightness or inevitability of this arrangement. This is often done by imposing a sense of inferiority.

The first step to changing this arrangement is a difficult one. There must come an acceptance of responsibility for complicity in one's present state of lack. One must rediscover self-love. A people who do not love themselves will insist upon nothing. They will make no humanizing demands upon themselves. Now must come acceptance of responsibility for one's purpose and destiny.

Wealth is More Than Money

Before delivering Israel from Egypt, God arranged a transfer of wealth that Israel might begin to construct a new destiny for themselves.

The Israelites did as Moses instructed and asked the Egyptians for articles of silver and gold and for clothing. The Lord had made the Egyptians favorably disposed toward the people, and they gave them what they asked for; so they plundered the Egyptians (Exodus 12:35,36, NIV).

After a series of plagues, the Egyptians gladly gave away their material possessions. The broad distribution of this wealth allowed each tribe and family among the Israelites to contribute to the task of building Moses' tabernacle.

God's perspective on wealth can be seen in a very important verse of Scripture. "But thou shalt remember the Lord thy God: for it is he that giveth thee power to get wealth, that he may establish his covenant which he sware unto thy fathers, as it is this day" (Deut. 8:18). Wealth is from the word *chayil* (khah-yil), meaning force, virtue, valor, strength, might, power, riches, substance, and valiant training. Power is firmness, vigor, force and capacity to produce; ability, might, strength, substance, and wealth. Wealth has more to do with ability, resources, and vision than with money.

God has given us wealth to get wealth. Until we exercise it, present conditions will not change. All the wasting potential must be rescued from crack houses, jails, orphanages, street corners, abortion clinics, liquor stores, gun shops, cigarettes, and unhealthy diets. The covenant God mentioned in the Book of Deuteronomy was one of compassion, dignity, and humanity. God said this optimal social arrangement needed wealth in order to be established.

Wealth can be the great liberator of human potential as wise use of it affords opportunities for the image of God in men and women.

God seemed to release wealth consistent with His desire to begin new things. Abraham received even more wealth after obeying God's leading to abandon familiar territory and strike out on the promise that a new people would spring from his loins. The Bible records Abraham as the first man to give tithes and to eat the bread and wine.

Tithe is an interesting word, meaning a tenth. Beyond this, however, the word literally means to accumulate, to grow or wax rich, to possess wealth and far richer riches. By tithing, Abraham set himself up to prosper in even greater measure.

What is the fundamental problem preventing many from becoming wealthy? I believe it's a misunderstanding of the purpose of wealth and/or a self-image not consistent with wealth and its attendant responsibility.

God does not have a problem with wealth. He is wealthy. Wealth is a gift from God that requires wise stewardship in order to accomplish the desire of God. Enough wealth exists for every citizen of the world to be a multi-millionaire.

While many in the church argue and dispute the theological implications of wealth, we fail to build compassionate, humanizing institutions. Every citizen should be liberated to achieve his or her potential, thus elevating the citizenry of this nation and world, strengthening its economies, and balancing the opportunity deficit. Communities could be rebuilt as renewed pride inflames the spirits of men, making them responsible for their environments.

One of my favorite Bible verses is Psalm 122:9. It reads, "For the sake of the house of the Lord our God, I will seek your prosperity" (NIV). Because of God's house and His desire to reach the nations with His salvation, David sought the financial benefits of God. The Hebrew word for seek is not passive. It means to search out in worship or prayer; to strive after, ask, beseech, desire, request, require, beg, or procure.

At this time in his life, David so desperately wanted to see salvation come to earth that he sought God diligently as to how he might prosper. When it was time to build the Temple of God under Solomon, David had come a long way from the poverty and obscurity of shepherding. From his personal treasury, David gave 120 tons of gold, 60 tons of silver, brass, and other precious building materials. This makes even the generosity of philanthropic John D. Rockefeller, who gave away $531,326,842 during his lifetime, pale in comparison.

When Work Has Meaning

The issue of meaningful work must arise when we discuss a people's potential for developing their wealth. Denis Waitley and Remi L. Witt in the prologue to *The Joy Working*, comment, "There can be no progress in the workplace until an individual values himself and feels valued by others. That's the foundation of all human fulfillment."

The Russian novelist Fyodor Dostoevsky wrote, "If it were desired to reduce a man to nothing, it would be necessary only to give his work a character of uselessness." Richard Lynch agreed, saying, "Man's work is an extension of himself, a revelation of his inner life, both to others and to himself."

Calvin Redekop and Urie A. Bender echoed that thought. They wrote, "As long as meaning is missing from work, our society will continue to experience more and more unhappiness."

What are the evidences of this unhappiness? We have 492,000 heroin junkies in the U.S., and authorities confiscate 224,712 pounds of cocaine in the U.S. each year. Every day in America a child under age 14 and 25 adults are murdered with handguns. Thirty three women endure the terror of rape; there are 575 robberies and 1,116 assaults. The United States — the murder and rape capital of the world — also ranks first in the number of deathrow inmates with 2,124. America leads the world with 22,520,000 marijuana users, far outstripping Australia, its closest competition with 703,100 reported users.

We need to look carefully at the causal factors involved with these statistics. I am positive that meaninglessness — not just related to work, but to life in general — is a strong contributing factor.

Is Money Sinful?

Many of us were left a legacy of hard work, but this work almost always profited someone besides ourselves. We inherited a rich spiritual legacy, but the church often told us that money was sinful. Ministers encouraged us to look forward to our rewards in heaven for the trials we endured on earth. But we can reap material and financial blessing in this life — and pass it on to our descendants. Our poverty mentality must yield to the reality that each human being is of inestimable personal worth and capable of developing vast wealth.

Some might object, saying, "Money will corrupt us and makes us less acceptable to God!" Let's examine that argument.

First, widespread corruption occurs in very poor areas, proving poverty and spirituality are not always synonymous. What about Abraham, Job, and Solomon — rich men in the Bible who were not only accepted by God, but in many cases were favored by Him? Some of our traditional thinking about wealth developed in order to ease the pain and despair of poverty. We may have given ourselves spiritual solace in the midst of poverty, but it can no longer be the prevailing mind-set.

We must also clear up our basic misconceptions about work if we intend to prosper and leave an inheritance to our children.

Ecclesiastes 3:13 says, "Every man should eat and drink, and enjoy the good of all his labour, it is the gift of God." God never intended work to be dehumanizing drudgery. God desires our labor to be a form of worship and self-actualization.

Live Up to Your Potential

America has the potential to be great for all its citizens, but our nation must be challenged to reach that potential. Everyone within our borders must be made to feel valuable and to experience the pride of achievement and accomplishment. Our churches must become concerned with the total lives of all persons. We must assist people in identifying their areas of calling, infusing them with passion and challenging them to be contributors and agents of renewal. This is prosperity, God-ness in all of life.

Proverbs 17:16 says, "Of what use is money in the hand of a fool, since he has no desire to get wisdom?" (NIV) Wisdom is essential. Seek it out. Read all you can in the area of calling God has chosen for you.

Americans spend 3.7 hours per week reading compared to 16 television viewing hours. Americans spend on average $30.85 per capita on books compared to $46.09 for Japanese and $119.61 for Norwegians. I suggest you spend more on books and audio and video teaching tapes. If this is not possible, then visit some of America's 11,529 libraries. Choose to become indispensable and so highly valued that you are an opportunity waiting to happen, potential waiting to explode.

Tell yourself, "I am incredible. I have God-given genius yet untapped. No one can stop me, and I will never, never, never give up!" Make everyone around you feel like a billion dollars. Squeeze, coax, cajole, or dynamite their potential out of them.

Don't listen to those who tell you it can't be done — the firehosers, the dream killers. Remember, most dream killers are people who at one time or another had their own dreams killed. Slap them, throw ice water on them, help them revive their dream, or get them involved with yours.

Choose to be productive. Become a tither and a great, big giver.

"Do just once what others say you can't do, and you will never pay attention to their limitations again," said James R. Cook. Overcoming their negative predictions will invigorate you. Walter Bagehot said, "The great pleasure in life is doing what people say you cannot do." Erica Jong said, "Everyone has talent. What is rare is the courage to follow the talent to the dark place where it leads."

Maybe you will be the 139th Nobel Prize winner for America in the sciences. Perhaps you'll be an inventor, joining the applicants who have filed nearly 105,000 requests for patents in the U.S. I am excited about your greatness. Arnold H. Glasow has said, "Progress is what happens when impossibility yields to necessity."

True Prosperity

We must become more responsible and wise with our wealth. We have been spending our wealth instead of investing it back into our communities. This must change immediately! Organizations within ethnic communities across America must begin to teach the responsibility for understanding and developing wealth. We must become producers. We must access and understand information and communications technology.

In the second letter to the Corinthians, the apostle Paul provides the secret to true prosperity:

[Remember] this: he who sows sparingly and grudgingly will also reap sparingly and grudgingly, and he who sows generously and that blessings may come to someone, will also reap generously and with blessings.

Let each one [give] as he has made up his own mind and purposed in his heart, not reluctantly or sorrowfully or under compulsion, for God loves (that is, He takes pleasure in, prizes above other things, and is unwilling to abandon or to do without) a cheerful (joyous, prompt-to-do-it) giver — whose heart is in his giving. [Proverbs 22:9]

And God is able to make all grace (every favor and earthly blessing) come to you in abundance, so that you may always and under all circumstances and whatever the need, be self-sufficient — possessing enough to require no aid or support and furnished in abundance for every good work and charitable donation.

As it is written, He [the benevolent person] scatters abroad, he gives to the poor; his deeds of justice and goodness and kindness and benevolence will go on and endure forever! [Psalm 112:9]

And [God] Who provides seed for the sower and bread for eating will also provide and multiply your [resources for] sowing, and increase the fruits of your righteousness [which manifests itself in active goodness, kindness and charity]. [Isa. 55:10; Hos.10:12]

Thus you will be enriched in all things and in every way, so that you can be generous, [and your generosity as it is] administered by us will bring forth thanksgiving to God (2 Cor. 9:6-11, Amplified).

Give all you can to the rebuilding of America's ghettos, barrios, and reservations. Invest in America's greatness. Romans 14:17 says, "For the kingdom of God is not meat and drink; but righteousness, and peace, and joy in the Holy Ghost." Righteousness essentially means the same as peace, an equitable social arrangement where justice dwells and universal prosperity is not only possible, but encouraged.

Joy is related to the Old Testament concept of shalom. It is the expression of delight over the prosperity, righteousness, and peace of God's kingdom where each person is valued, contributing, and reaching his full potential. This is worship. This is the kingdom of God. This is true prosperity!

Leaving a Legacy

Many of our ancestors abandoned their dreams and settled for a life of poverty and mediocrity. Don't misunderstand me. Many were men and women of tremendous integrity and principle. They simply did not see themselves as capable of making millions and wisely investing it so that their children and grandchildren would benefit. Solomon said, "A good man leaveth an inheritance to his children's children: and the wealth of the sinner is laid up for the just" (Prov. 13:22).

Inheritance comes from the Hebrew word *nachal* (naw-khal), which means to occupy, bequeath, distribute, or instate. The verb form of *nachal* occurs 60 times in the Old Testament and connotes the giving or receiving of property that has been a permanent possession and is the result of succession. In other words, this property has been in the family for generations. This family understands the law of use and has gained a profit from its substance, which perpetuates the Lord's blessing upon this family. This good man has an inheritance laid up for his grandchildren.

This principle is found throughout Scripture. Abraham left an inheritance of wealth to Isaac, Isaac to Jacob, and Jacob to his sons and grandsons. David transferred great wealth to his sons. Remember that wealth is more than money or income. Wealth is not only your cumulative assets that make money for you but also the ability, genius, and ingenuity to transform ideas into more wealth.

Teaching Our Children to Succeed

We must begin to teach our children about their miracle potential and of their capacity to generate wealth. They must also be taught that great responsibility rests upon the shoulders of a wealthy man or woman. The Bible declares, "unto whomsoever much is given, of him shall be much required" (Luke 12:48). This is true both before and after the fact.

If God has given you many ideas, you have a tremendous responsibility to bring as many ideas as possible to fruition. I have heard it said that success breeds success. Many of us have not yet begun to prosper because we have not pursued the dreams in our hearts.

We must discover the keys to success and profitability, then pass them on to our offspring. We must challenge them to discover and use every ounce of their potential.

We have an obligation to teach our children the ways of God, but we also must nourish their own genius and set them on course toward the heroic and the noble. They must be taught persistence and insistence. Our children must be taught to properly care for their possessions and to groom and excellently care for their own spirits, minds, and bodies. Our youth must be taught to grasp broad concepts and master specific skills. We must teach them to write and to speak confidently and articulately.

Every human being is born successful. Somehow, somewhere, however, we learned to become negative, self-doubting, and retiring. Our children must be taught to take responsibility for their own lives, for the decisions they make, for the paths they choose.

Just as Mrs. Sonya Carson did with her sons Benjamin and Curtis, we must challenge our children to draw upon the deepest levels of their abilities and leave something great and memorable to the world. Even though Mrs. Carson made tremendous sacrifices to singularly raise her sons in the ghettos of Detroit, she never instilled the ghetto in them. They were in the ghetto, but the ghetto was not in them.

One of the greatest things any human can do is to succeed in spite of dreary, unpromising circumstances. Block out the jeers and cat calls of those who write you off as a loser. The triumph of rising from past failures, overcoming debilitating habits, and exceeding someone's limited expectations of you is exhilarating.

Compassion calls us to look beyond ourselves. We must teach our children — by first setting for them an example — to be committed to the success of all human beings. Encouraging others to reach their potential has its own special reward.

Reaching Your Genius Potential

We must understand that we owe God and we owe humanity. Someone once said, "Our talents and abilities are God's gift to us; what we do with them is our gift to God."

Remember:

1. Know God

2. Strive to be a person of character

3. Practice the life of prayer and pray big prayers

4. Eat healthy foods and get regular exercise

5. Value knowledge, wisdom, and expertise

6. Never, never, never give up

7. Commit yourself to excellence

8. Seek to prosper in all you do

9. Leave a legacy

10. Love and greatly esteem others

I've enjoyed sharing these thoughts with you. I offer them as a gift, as seed sown toward your success. I sincerely pray that you will discover the beautiful person that God has made you to be.

May you prosper and experience God's love and joy in all of life.

Everyone is special and unique! Everyone has genius potential. You must use it or lose it!

May you tap into your God-given genius, reach your full potential, and realize your every dream. I know you can do it!

Notes

Notes

Notes

Notes

The African Cultural Heritage Topical Bible

The African Cultural Heritage Topical Bible is a quick and convenient reference Bible. It has been designed for use in personal devotions as well as group Bible studies. It's the newest and most complete reference Bible designed to reveal the Black presence in the Bible and highlight the contributions and exploits of Blacks from the past to present. It's a great tool for students, clergy, teachers — practically anyone seeking to learn more about the Black presence in Scripture, but didn't know where to start.

The African Cultural Heritage Topical Bible contains:
- Over **395** easy to find **topics**
- **3,840 verses** that are systematically organized
- A comprehensive listing of Black inventions
- Over **150 pages** of Christian Afrocentric articles on Blacks in the Bible, Contributions of Africa, African Foundations of Christianity, Culture, Identity, Leadership, and Racial Reconciliation written by Myles Munroe, Wayne Perryman, Dr. Leonard Lovett, Dr. Trevor L. Grizzle, James Giles, and Dr. Mensa Otabil.

Available in KJV and NIV versions

Why?
by T.D. Jakes

Why do the righteous, who have committed their entire lives to obeying God, seem to endure so much pain and experience such conflict? These perplexing questions have plagued and bewildered Christians for ages. In this anointed and inspirational new book, Bishop T.D. Jakes provocatively and skillfully answers these questions and many more as well as answering the "why" of the anointed.

Why? Workbook
by T.D. Jakes

WHY? Workbook will help you to understand and overcome the difficulties that surround your life. Over 150 thought provoking questions will help you discover answers to the "whys" in your own life. Designed with a user friendly, cutting edge study system and answer key, it is an exciting and powerful tool for individual group studies.

Water in the Wilderness
by T.D. Jakes

Just before you apprehend your greatest conquest, expect the greatest struggle. Many are perplexed who encounter this season of adversity. This book will show you how to survive the worst of times with the greatest of ease, and will cause fountains of living water to spring out of the parched, sun–drenched areas in your life. This word is a refreshing stream in the desert for the weary traveler.

The Harvest
by T.D. Jakes

Have you been sidetracked by Satan? Are you preoccupied with the things of this world? Are you distracted by one crisis after another? You need to get your act together before it's too late! God's strategy for the end-time harvest is already set in motion. Phase One is underway, and Phase Two is close behind. If you don't want to be left behind tomorrow, you need to take action today. With startling insight, T.D. Jakes sets the record straight. You'll be shocked to learn how God is separating people into two distinct categories. One thing is certain – after reading *The Harvest,* you'll know exactly where you stand with God. This book will help you discover who will and who won't be included in the final ingathering and determine what it takes to be prepared. If you miss *The Harvest,* you'll regret it for all eternity!

Help Me! I've Fallen
by T.D. Jakes

"Help! I've fallen, and I can't get up." This cry, made popular by a familiar television commercial, points out the problem faced by many Christians today. Have you ever stumbled and fallen with no hope of getting up? Have you been wounded and hurt by others? Are you so far down you think you'll never stand again? Don't despair. All Christians fall from time to time. Life knocks us off balance, making it hard – if not impossible – to get back on our feet. The cause of the fall is not as important as what we do while we're down. T.D. Jakes explains how – and Whom – to ask for help. In a struggle to regain your balance, this book is going to be your manual to recovery! Don't panic. This is just a test!

When Shepherds Bleed
by T.D. Jakes

Shepherding is a dangerous profession, and no one knows that better than a pastor. Drawing from personal encounters with actual shepherds in Israel and years of ministry, Bishop T.D. Jakes and Stanley Miller provide unique insight into the hazards faced by pastors today. With amazing perception, the authors pull back the bandages and uncover the open, bleeding wounds common among those shepherding God's flock. Using the skills of spiritual surgeons, they precisely cut to the heart of the problem and tenderly apply the cure. You'll be moved to tears as your healing process begins. Open your heart and let God lead you beside the still waters where He can restore your soul.

Becoming A Leader
by Myles Munroe

Many consider leadership to be no more than staying ahead of the pack, but that is a far cry from what leadership is. Leadership is deploying others to become as good as or better than you are. Within each of us lies the potential to be an effective leader. *Becoming A Leader* uncovers the secrets of dynamic leadership that will show you how to be a leader in your family, school, community, church and on your job. No matter where you are or what you do in life, this book can help you to inevitably become a leader. Remember: it is never too late to become a leader. As in every tree there is a forest, so in every follower there is a leader.

Becoming A Leader Workbook
by Myles Munroe

Now you can activate your leadership potential through the *Becoming A Leader Workbook*. This workbook has been designed to take you step by step through the leadership principles taught in *Becoming A Leader*. As you participate in the work studies you will see the true leader inside you develop and grow into maturity. ***"Knowledge with action produces results."***

This is My Story
by Candi Staton

This is My Story is a touching autobiography about a gifted young child who rose from obscurity and poverty to stardom and wealth. With a music career that included selling millions of albums and topping the charts came a life of brokenness, loneliness, and despair. This book will make you cry and laugh as you witness one woman's search for success and love.

The God Factor
by James Giles

Is something missing in your life? Do you find yourself at the mercy of your circumstances? Is your self-esteem at an all-time low? Are your dreams only a faded memory? You could be missing the one element that could make the difference between success and failure, poverty and prosperity, and creativity and apathy. Knowing God supplies the creative genius you need to reach your potential and realize your dream. You'll be challenged as James Giles shows you how to tap into your God-given genius, take steps toward reaching your goal, pray big and get answers, eat right and stay healthy, prosper economically and personally, and leave a lasting legacy for your children.

Making the Most of Your Teenage Years
by David Burrows

Most teenagers live for today. Living only for today, however, can kill you. When teenagers have no plan for their future, they follow a plan that someone else devised. Unfortunately, this plan often leads them to drugs, sex, crime, jail, and an early death. How can you make the most of your teenage years? Discover who you really are – and how to plan for the three phases of your life. You can develop your skill, achieve your dreams, and still have fun.

Strategies for Saving the Next Generation
by Dave Burrows

This book will teach you how to start and effectively operate a vibrant youth ministry. This book is filled with practical tips and insight gained over a number of years working with young people from the street to the parks to the church. Dave Burrows offers the reader vital information that will produce results if carefully considered and adapted. It's excellent for pastors and youth pastors as well as youth workers and those involved with youth ministry.

Five Years To Life
by Sam Huddleston

One day in jail, Sam's life changed. He writes, "Jesus used my daddy, not to scare the hell out of me, but to love it out of me." *Five Years To Life* is the moving account of the power of unconditional love from an earthly father and from the heavenly Father. It's the story of a man who learned to make right choices because his heart had been dramatically changed.

The Biblical Principles of Success
Arthur L. Mackey Jr.

There are only three types of people in the world: 1) People who make things happen, 2) People who watch things happen, and 3) People who do not know what in the world is happening. *The Biblical Principles of Success* will help you become one who makes things happen. Success is not a matter of "doing it my way." It is turning from a personal, selfish philosophy to God's outreaching, sharing way of life. This powerful book teaches you how to tap into success principles that are guaranteed – *the Biblical principles of success!*

Flaming Sword
by Tai Ikomi

Scripture memorization and meditation bring tremendous spiritual power, however many Christians find it to be an uphill task. Committing Scriptures to memory will transform the mediocre Christian to a spiritual giant. This book will help you to become addicted to the powerful practice of Scripture memorization and help you obtain the victory that you desire in every area of your life. *Flaming Sword* is your pathway to spiritual growth and a more intimate relationship with God.

Four Laws of Productivity
by Dr. Mensa Otabil

Success has no favorites, but it does have associates. Success will come to anyone who will pay the price to receive its benefits. *Four Laws of*

Productivity will give you the powerful keys that will help you achieve your life's goals. You will learn how to discover God's gift in you, develop your gift, perfect your gift, and utilize your gift to its maximum potential. The principles revealed in this timely book will radically change your life.

Beyond the Rivers of Ethiopia

by Mensa Otabil

Beyond the Rivers of Ethiopia is a powerful and revealing look into God's purpose for the Black race. It gives scholastic yet simple answers to questions you have always had about the Black presence in the Bible. At the heart of this book is a challenge and call to the offspring of the Children of Africa, both on the continent and throughout the world, to come to grips with their true identity as they go *Beyond the Rivers of Ethiopia.*

Single Life

by Earl D. Johnson

A book that candidly addresses the spiritual and physical dimensions of the single life is finally here. *Single Life* shows the reader how to make their singleness a celebration rather than a burden. This positive approach to singles uses enlightening examples from Apostle Paul, himself a single, to beautifully portray the dynamic aspects of the single life by serving the Lord more effectively. The book gives fresh insight on practical issues such as coping with sexual desires, loneliness, and preparation for your future mate. Written in a lively style, the author admonishes singles to seek first the kingdom of God and rest assured in God's promise to supply their needs... including a life partner!

Leadership in the New Testament Church

by Earl D. Johnson

Leadership in the New Testament Church offers practical and applicable insight into the role of leadership in the present day church. In this book, the author explains the qualities that leaders must have, explores the interpersonal relationships between the leader and his staff, the leader's influence in the church and society, and how to handle conflicts that arise among leaders.

The Call of God
by Jefferson Edwards

Since I have been called to preach, now what? Many sincere Christians are confused about their call to the ministry. Some are zealous and run ahead of their time and season of training and preparation while others are behind their time neglecting the gift of God within them. *The Call of God* gives practical instruction for pastors and leaders to refine and further develop their ministry and tips on how to nourish and develop others with God's call to effectively proclaim the gospel of Christ. *The Call of God* will help you to • Have clarity from God as to what ministry involves • Be able to identify and affirm the call in your life • See what stage you are in your call from God • Remove confusion in relation to the processing of a call or the making of the person • Understand the development of the anointing to fulfill your call.

Gifted
by Jefferson Edwards

In this book, you will gain fresh appreciation for the roles blacks played even in welcoming the King of glory to our cosmos. It is a call to the Black race to reach deep into their treasures and discover, develop and with excellence release their gift to the King of Kings.

Come, Let Us Pray
by Emmette Weir

Are you satisfied with your prayer life? Are you finding that your prayers are often dull, repetitive and lacking in spiritual power? Are you looking for ways to improve your relationship with God? Would you like to be able to pray more effectively? Then *Come, Let Us Pray* will help you in these areas and more. If you want to gain the maximum spiritual experience from your prayer life and enter into the very presence of God – *Come, Let Us Pray.*

Mobilizing Human Resources
by Richard Pinder

Pastor Pinder gives an in-depth look at how to organize, motivate, and deploy members of the Body of Christ in a manner that produces maximum effect for your ministry. This book will assist you in organizing and motivating your troops for effective and efficient ministry. It will also help the individual believer in recognizing their place in the body, using their God given abilities and talents to maximum effect.

The Layman's Guide to Counseling

by Susan Wallace

The increasing need for counseling has caused today's Christian leaders to become more sensitive to raise up lay-counselors to share this burden with them. Jesus' command is to "set the captives free." *The Layman's Guide to Counseling* shows you how. A number of visual aids in the form of charts, lists, and tables are also integrated into this reference book: the most comprehensive counseling tool available. *The Layman's Guide to Counseling* gives you the knowledge you need to use advanced principles of Word-based counseling to equip you to be effective in your counseling ministry. **Topics Include** • Inner Healing • Parenting • Marriage • Deliverance • Abuse • Forgiveness • Drug & Alcohol Recovery • Youth Counseling • Holy Spirit • Premarital Counseling

The 1993 Trial on the Curse of Ham

by Wayne Perryman

Is the Black race cursed? Over 450 people attended this trial. It was the first time in <u>over</u> **3,000 years** that Ham had an opportunity to tell his side of the story and explain exactly what took place in the tent of his father, Noah. The evidence submitted by the defense on behalf of Ham and his descendants was so powerful that it **shocked** the audience and **stunned** the jury. Evidence presented by the defense was supported by **over 442 biblical references**.

The Church

by Turnel Nelson

Discover God's true intent and purpose for His Church in this powerful new release by Pastor Turnel Nelson. This book speaks to the individual with an exciting freshness and urgency to become the true Bride of Christ.

Opening the Front Door of Your Church

by Dr. Leonard Lovett

A creative approach for small to medium churches who want to develop a more effective ministry. *Opening the Front Door Of Your Church* is an insightful and creative approach to church development and expansion, especially for churches within the urban environment.

Another Look at Sex
by Charles Phillips
This book is undoubtedly a head turner and eye opener that will cause you to take another close look at sex. In this book, Charles Phillips openly addresses this seldom discussed subject and gives life-changing advice on sex to married couples and singles. If you have questions about sex, this is the book for you.

The Minister's Topical Bible
by Derwin Stewart
The Minister's Topical Bible covers every aspect of the ministry providing quick and easy access to scriptures in a variety of ministry related topics. This handy reference tool can be effectively used in leadership training, counseling, teaching, sermon preparation, and personal study.

The Believer's Topical Bible
by Derwin Stewart
The Believer's Topical Bible covers every aspect of a Christian's relationship with God and man, providing biblical answers and solutions for many challenges. It is a quick, convenient, and thorough reference Bible that has been designed for use in personal devotions and group Bible studies. With over 3,800 verses systematically organized under 240 topics, it is the largest devotional-topical Bible available in the New International Version and the King James Version.

God's Glorious Outpouring *(Video)*
A must-see for every Christian leader.
HOSTED BY: Tim Storey, Leon Isaac Kennedy and Carlton Pearson. In 1906, within a former horse stable, then converted into Azusa Missions, ordinary people met with an extraordinary God! Relive this outpouring which has been termed by church scholars as God's greatest outpouring of the 20th Century! Listen as today's outstanding church historians Dr. Vinson Synan, Dr. Cecil Roebeck, and others relate how this outpouring swept throughout the world and has now encompassed over 350 million people! Reflect as the only known witnesses relate how it really was! Be

inspired as those who were there tell how the Lord is. He will soon do it again!

Tragedy to Triumph *(Video)*

He dared to follow God. The results – he was a catalyst that helped change the world! A must-see for every Christian leader. HOSTED BY: Tim Storey and Leon Isaac Kennedy. Most have never heard of William Seymour, yet Yale Church historian Sydney Ahlstrom remarks, "Seymour exerted a greater influence upon American Christianity than any other black leader." Within one year, not only the United States but fifty other nations were touched as 312 Azusa Street became one of the most famous addresses in the world! Listen as today's outstanding church historians Dr. Vinson Synan, Dr. Leonard Lovett, former presiding Bishop Ford of the Church of God in Christ, Dr. Cecil Roebeck, Jim Zieglar and others relate how this outpouring swept throughout the world and has now encompassed over 350 million people!

All these books are available at your local bookstore or by contacting:

Pneuma Life Publishing
P.O. Box 10612
Bakersfield, CA 93389-0612

1-800-727-3218
1-805-324-1741